Wild, Wild World of Animals

Fishes
of Lakes, Rivers & Oceans

A TIME-LIFE TELEVISION BOOK

Editor: Charles Osborne
Text Editor: Richard Oulahan
   Associate Text Editor: Bonnie Johnson
   Author: Thomas A. Dozier
   Writers: Deborah Heineman, Cecilia Waters
   Literary Research: Ellen Schachter
   Text Research: Mary Jane Hodges
   Copy Editors: Eleanor Van Bellingham, Robert Braine
Picture Editor: Richard O. Pollard
   Picture Research: Judith Greene
   Permissions and Production: Cecilia Waters
Designer: Constance A. Timm
   Art Assistant: Carl Van Brunt
Production Editor: Joan Chambers

WILD, WILD WORLD OF ANIMALS
TELEVISION PROGRAM
Producers: Jonathan Donald and Lothar Wolff
This Time-Life Television book is published by Time-Life Films, Inc.
Bruce L. Paisner, *President*
J. Nicoll Durrie, *Vice President*

THE AUTHOR

THOMAS A. DOZIER was a foreign correspondent for *Time* and *Life* magazines for 24 years and has also written for *Sports Illustrated, Smithsonian* and *Travel and Camera* magazines. He is the author of two other volumes in this series, *Whales & Other Sea Mammals* and *Dangerous Sea Creatures*, the co-author of *Life in the Coral Reef*, and a contributor to *Land Giants* and *The Cats*.

THE CONSULTANTS

C. LAVETT SMITH is Curator and Chairman of the Department of Ichthyology at the American Museum of Natural History in New York. His research interests include the community ecology of coral reef fish and the ichthyofauna of New York State. As a diver-scientist he has studied fish in the Caribbean Sea and the Pacific and Indian oceans.

DR. JAMES W. ATZ is a Curator of the Department of Ichthyology at the American Museum of Natural History in New York.

THE COVER: A male salmon displays the typical humped back and bright-pink coloration of a spawning sockeye. During its upstream migration from the ocean to the river spawning grounds, the sockeye's scales are absorbed, its body—in peak condition—compresses and its olive-green snout develops a sharply curving, elongated hook.

Fishes
of Lakes, Rivers & Oceans

Based on the television series
Wild, Wild World of Animals

Published by
TIME-LIFE FILMS

© 1978 Time-Life Films, Inc. All rights reserved.

ISBN 0-913948-20-9

Library of Congress Catalog Card Number: 78-51971

Printed in the United States of America.

Contents

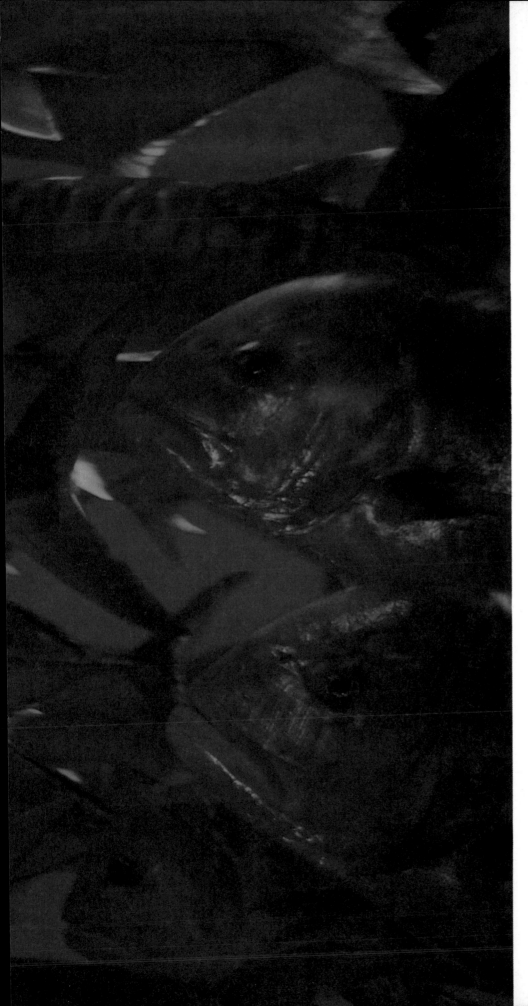

Introduction
by *Thomas A. Dozier*

WHEN HE WAS A YOUNG PRINCE, 15 or 16 years old, Alexander the Great reportedly descended under the sea, in a strange contraption of glass bound with metal rings, to observe—and presumably to be observed by—the creatures there. What Alexander thought, in his primitive diving bell, is not recorded, but he apparently decided to leave the realm of the sea to Poseidon and set out to conquer other, more terrestrial worlds.

The watery world has always awed and excited men, as well it might, for it is an awesome, exciting place, almost as mysterious today as it was in the time of Alexander. It is a realm where the statistics are measured in superlatives. Seven-tenths of the earth's surface is covered by water. All life on earth—all creatures of the land, sea and air—had its origin in the water. The water itself is truly a life-giving elixir; moreover, without it no life as it is presently conceived could continue, and the earth would become as dead as the moon.

The watery world is a place of endless changing environments with as many hazards and obstacles as any terrestrial habitat, along with the added pressures of a medium with 800 times the density of air. A number of reptiles, amphibians, mammals and birds have returned to the water their ancestors emerged from, retaining only the most tenuous connections with the land; others, notably the whales and the sea snakes, have severed all terrestrial connections, living, breeding and dying in the sea; and still others, such as polar bears and penguins, are in the process of becoming completely aquatic. Yet the creatures that are the unquestioned masters of their element, that never left it, are the fishes.

Like almost everything else about the world's bodies of water and the creatures that live within them, the fishes must be described in superlative terms. An extinct fish, a jawless, armored member of the ancient class Agnatha, was the first vertebrate and the seed ancestor of all amphibians, reptiles, fishes, birds and mammals, including man. Fishes are the most numerous of all living vertebrate species: more than 20,000 different species are known and as many more may still be undiscovered, more in any case than all other bony-skeletoned creatures put together. The fishes are, with the exception of the myriad insects, the most prolific of living creatures. A single female codfish may lay as many as two to nine million eggs in one spawning. At the same time, the actuarial tables for fishes are among the lowest in the world—a good thing, for if by some miracle every single egg that was spawned in the waters of the world in one breeding season was able to survive to become an adult fish, the oceans would very quickly be displaced and the planet smothered by trillions of fishes. Ichthyologists consider that a salmon spawning is successful, for instance, if just two of the 5,000-odd eggs laid by a female and fertilized by a male should reach maturity.

In their world of water, fishes are nearly ubiquitous, inhabiting almost every environment and adapting to the most difficult conditions. The Alaskan blackfish lives where the water is frigid, and it can survive being immobilized in a block of ice. The pupfish, on the other hand, lives in waters of 120° F. The more hospitable waters of a temperate creek may harbor two or three piscine

This illuminated page from The Hours of Catherine of Cleves *portrays St. Lawrence, patron of the poor, and gives the beginning of a prayer to him. Around the border of the page and on some of the floor tiles, fish are shown eating fish, symbolizing a popular allegorical theme of 15th and 16th century literature: the poor being devoured by the rich.*

Sanctissime ac beatissime martir laurenti. supplicater ego peccator seruus tuus pietatem tuam exoro vt pro me spurcissimo multis q̃ viciorum ponderibz oppresso preces effundere digneris ad omnipotentem deum quatinus

environments, with catfish scavenging the bottom, pikes lurking in the shoreline reeds, smallmouth bass occupying the cool, well-oxygenated upper reaches, largemouth bass in the more tepid lower reaches, and minnows filling in the niches in between and incidentally providing food for the larger fishes. The great rivers and tributary streams are highways of migration for those fishes that move from one environment to another: the catadromous fish (meaning "down runners"), such as eels, which are born in the sea, move to freshwater streams and return to the ocean as adults to spawn; and the more numerous anadromous (from the Greek for "up runners"), salmon, shad, certain trout and others, which reverse the migratory pattern, moving from the mountain streams where they were born to the ocean and back again years later to spawn and often to die.

The estuaries are crossroads for the wanderers, where the sea and the inland waters meet. Beyond, in coastal and coral seas, live most of the world's fishes, great navies of schooling bluefish, striped bass, herrings, anchovies and other species that darken the seas as far as the eye can see, then abruptly disappear, bound for unknown destinations for unknown reasons. A classic case of the disappearing acts of coastal fishes is that of the striped bass. In the years following the Civil War, this bass inhabited the eastern littoral of the United States in seemingly limitless numbers. They became the special perquisite of wealthy sportsmen who established exclusive bass-fishing clubs, which reportedly furnished the members with carrier pigeons for sending instructions to their New York offices. In 1900, the stripers mysteriously vanished from their northeastern habitats and did not return again for 30 years, by which time they were fair game for all fishermen.

The blue water of the oceans is the preserve of the monsters of the sea—whale sharks, the largest of all fish, which may weigh more than 20 tons and measure 70 feet, giant tunas, groupers, marlins and swordfish. These share the ocean expanses with whales and giant squids and other nonpiscine creatures as well as smaller pelagic fish, vast schools of herring, mackerel and flying fish.

Deeper in the sea, in the twilight zone (from 600 to 3,200 feet), dwell the bathypelagic fishes, generally primitive, small (six inches or less) silvery creatures, most of which are equipped with phosphorescent lighting organs, which probably serve as means of recognizing species and for locating a mate in the murky darkness. A few extraordinary fishes dwell in the abyssal zone at depths as low as 35,000 feet, where the pressure is extreme, the temperature low and no light ever penetrates. These strange fishes are somewhat elongated—reaching a foot or more—but curiously only one group has a light organ. Three groups, the rattails, halosaurs and notocanths, have special tails for locating food in the ocean bottom. Says one authority: "Deep-sea fishes . . . are essentially weightless . . . owning no niches and having no homes, are endless wanderers in a ceaselessly moving domain. Deep-sea fish are weak swimmers. Perhaps there is no reason to go anywhere in this endless sameness."

The oceanic deeps continue to hide many mysteries that sometimes surface to tantalize scientists: As recently as 1938, fishermen in the Indian Ocean off the coast of Africa trawled a grotesque fish with armlike fins. It proved to be a coelacanth, a primitive "living fossil," which ichthyologists had presumed to be extinct for 60 million years and which is related to the progenitor of terrestrial animals and man. Since then, dozens of other catches have confirmed the fact that the ancient fish lives on.

The illustration above is from a 15th century manuscript in the Musée de Condé in Chantilly, France. It depicts a youthful Alexander the Great in his makeshift bathysphere surveying the wonders of the deep. The illustration is captioned, "How Alexander had himself lowered in a glass container to the sea-bed."

Of the known fishes, 10,000 species live in fresh waters; others, numbering 15,000 or more species, are creatures of the seas. There are two principal classes of extant fishes: Chondrichthyes, the sharks, rays, skates and chimaeras, which are true vertebrates although their internal skeletons are composed almost entirely of lightweight cartilage; and Osteichthyes, the bony fish, which comprise 90 per cent of all fishes, with skeletons of true bone. A third, ancient, related class, Agnatha, the jawless fishes, has just two living forms: the eel-like lampreys and the hagfish, bottom-dwelling scavengers that resemble worms.

In adapting to their many varied environments, fishes have assumed fantastic shapes and acquired skills and weapons that are the equal of anything evolved by terrestrial animals. Most fishes filter oxygen through gills and have scaled bodies, but there are many exceptions, like climbing perch and mudskippers, that breathe by means of lungs or lunglike sacs and even walk around on the land. Others are armored with bony plates, like sturgeons, bristling with spines, like some puffers, or have no scaly covering at all, like some catfish. In general, bottom fish are flattened and camouflaged to resemble vegetation or rocks, and fishes that inhabit higher levels are streamlined, with forked tails to facilitate moving through water and against currents. Some stalking predators, like barracudas and pikes, have elongated, torpedo shapes and are equipped with formidable teeth designed to strike at their prey in lightninglike thrusts. Others, such as bluegills and angelfish, are no more than vertically flattened, finned disks, fashioned for easy movement through reeds and other vegetation where they feed and hide. Some are marvelously colored. The dolphin (not to be confused with the marine mammal of the same name) is a dazzling rainbow of different hues; perhaps the most beautiful of all

Fish
Evolution

AGNATHA (jawless fishes)

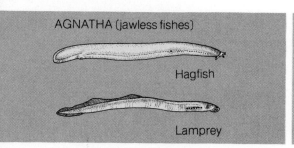

Hagfish

Lamprey

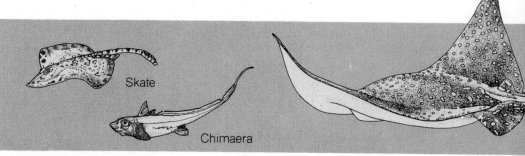

Skate

Chimaera

OSTEICHTHYES (ray-finned bony fishes)

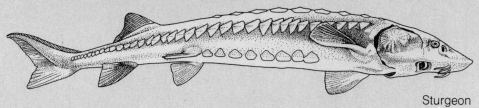

Sturgeon

Bichir

Gar

Bowfin

TELEOSTS

Eel

Bonefish

Herring

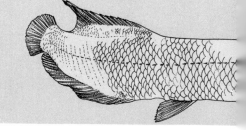

Bullhead

Cod

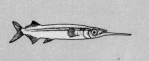

Halfbeak

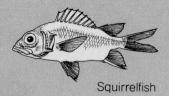

Squirrelfish

Cabezon

Perch

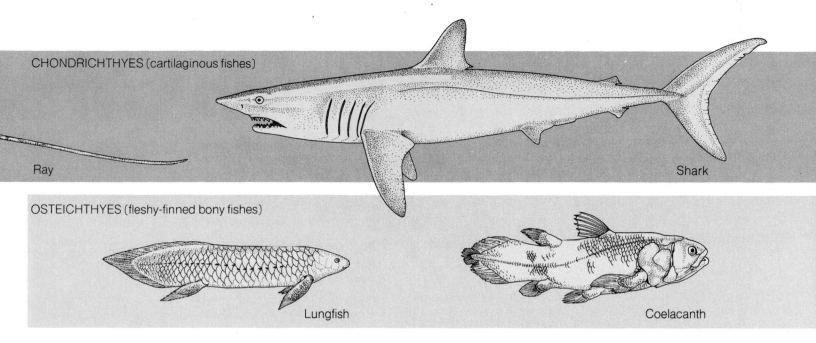

CHONDRICHTHYES (cartilaginous fishes)

Ray

Shark

OSTEICHTHYES (fleshy-finned bony fishes)

Lungfish

Coelacanth

The most primitive of living fishes, shown above and at left on a blue background, relate to ancestral forms that evolved from invertebrate creatures of the sea. The oldest class, Agnatha, or jawless fishes, the lampreys and hagfishes, evolved a simple, jawless mouth for sucking in food, gills for oxygen intake and a skimpy fin for mobility. Somewhat more advanced are the Chondrichthyes, or cartilaginous fishes, the rays, skates and sharks, and the related chimaeras, which acquired skeletons of gristle, as well as jaws and teeth, and planelike paired fins to ensure balance and stability. Lacking the buoyancy provided by swim bladders or lungs of more modern fishes, the cartilaginous fishes

must keep swimming constantly or sink to the bottom. The earliest Osteichthyes, bony fishes—sturgeons, gars, bichirs, bowfins, paddlefish—developed some hydrostatic control and consequent maneuverability along with their partially ossified skeletons and more elaborate fin formations. The powerful lobed fins of the coelacanth are capable of crawling—marking that ancient fish as a distant forerunner of four-limbed reptiles, amphibians, mammals and, eventually, man. The large size of so many of the primitive fishes harks back to the time when the oceans were relatively empty regions and there was an infinite watery space to grow and roam in.

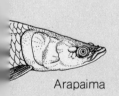

Arapaima

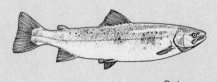

Salmon

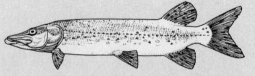

Muskellunge

Viperfish

The modern fishes, depicted against a green background, are all teleosts—true bony fish, with skeletons of lightweight bone, and symmetrical tails. Carps, catfishes and minnows, the dominant fish of the world's fresh waters, even have a special series of ear bones that provide them with acute hearing. With the development of a swim bladder, teleosts have achieved weightlessness and with flexible fin rays a talent for precise maneuvering. The older teleosts, like herrings and salmons, have a single dorsal fin, and pelvic fins well behind the pectoral fins. The cods and their relatives sprout a full complement of as many as 10 fins, with the pelvics projecting from the throat. Sharp, protective spines

appear first in the fins of the squirrelfish group; cabezons bristle with spiny fins, which in many species are venomous. The perchlike fishes have paired fins set close together that function for fast maneuvering. The wahoo, a member of the mackerel-tuna family, is a silhouette of speed, with its slender, deeply forked tail and two rows of streamlined finlets. Two extreme adaptations are the flatfishes, characterized by the pancake-shaped flounder with both eyes placed surrealistically on its upper side, and the cowfish, a feeble swimmer encased in a box of fused plates—and surprisingly good to eat when it is properly cooked in its "shell."

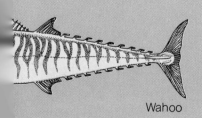

Wahoo

Halibut

Cowfish

⊢——⊣
1'

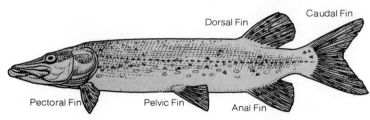

Dorsal Fin Caudal Fin

Pectoral Fin Pelvic Fin Anal Fin

Muskellunge

A fish's fins serve a twofold purpose: They provide propulsion and help the fish maintain equilibrium. The median fins, on the back (dorsal) and the abdomen (anal), prevent the fish from rolling over. Two sets of paired fins, the pelvics and the pectorals, prevent pitching and help the fish steer. Yaw—the tendency to swerve sideways—is negligible in long-bodied fish like the muskellunge (above), but short-bodied fish like the bluegill (below) need a large expanse of dorsal fin to stay on course. To move forward a fish first jets water from the gills, flexes the body and then beats the caudal fin, which in active fish provides most of the propulsive power.

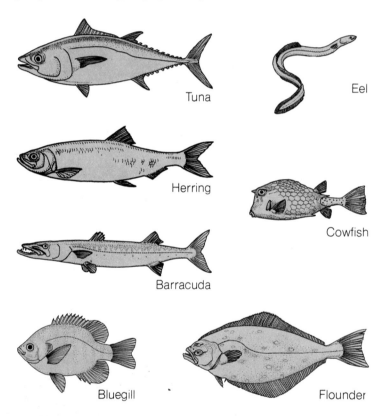

Tuna

Eel

Herring

Cowfish

Barracuda

Bluegill

Flounder

The different shapes of fishes' bodies reveal much about their way of life. Migratory pelagic fish, like the tuna and herring, have streamlined spindle shapes with lunate or deeply forked tails. Torpedo-shaped fish such as the barracuda, gar and pike have dorsal and anal fins clustered near the tail like the feathers of an arrow, enabling them to hover in the shallows and lunge at prey. Such flattened fishes as the bluegill and halibut have extensive median fins and a squarish tail for short bursts of speed. Eels are elongated to suit them for life in rocky crevices or in ooze, and they move by undulating their median fins and their bodies. The box-shaped cowfishes drift rather than swim.

fishes, it turns a drab gray when it dies. The golden trout, a native of mountain lakes of the High Sierras, has the striking gold and scarlet colors of a Spanish flag, but it quickly hybridizes with other trout and loses its colors. By contrast, some fishes are virtually invisible. A species of goby, *Pandaka pygmaea*, a tiny denizen of freshwater streams and lakes of the Philippines, is not only the world's smallest vertebrate (adults grow no longer than one half inch), it is almost transparent. Young eels are even less visible: On an excursion to the Sargasso Sea, where all the world's eels are born, William Beebe, the famous naturalist, described a young eel he held in his hand as "a twelve-inch piece of flexible water. There was absolutely no structure to be seen except the gleaming eyes, and yet here was a living fish."

Many fishes have acquired taste buds on their fins, tails and other odd parts of their bodies to locate food easily. Some have remarkable eye modifications. One hatchetfish gazes up through the gloom of the sea with eyes that are tubular appendages; certain blennies are equipped with bifocal eyes that have two "windows" in the cornea, one for spotting insects in the air at the water's surface, the other for navigating underwater. In the evolutionary process, some fishes have developed formidable weapons—teeth that can swiftly reduce a body to polished bones, venomous fins, stinging spines and electric shock charges that could kill a man or stun a horse, and poisonous flesh that causes agonizing death if eaten. In all their forms, shapes, colors and weaponry, fishes surpass the most fanciful bestiary creatures created by men.

As the oldest of all vertebrates, fishes have inhabited the waters of the earth for upward of 440 million years. By comparison, *Homo sapiens* is a mere infant of 40,000 years, newly arrived on an ancient stage. Yet man has proved to be the greatest enemy of the creatures of the sea, as predator, despoiler of environments and well-intentioned but often inept manager. The meddling of humans in what is essentially an alien environment has often upset very delicate balances and created disasters. Man-made canals opened up the Great Lakes to sea lampreys, which very quickly decimated the lake trout in Lake Superior. The rainbow trout that were introduced to

Lake Titicaca, high in the Andes, all but killed off all the indigenous *orestias*, an important food fish of the region, in less than a decade. Alewives, invading Lake Michigan through the Welland Canal, multiplied by the millions, snuffing out the trouts and other native fishes and even exterminating themselves in their great numbers so that they piled up in rotting shoals on the beaches of the inland sea. (The coho salmon, introduced in 1966, finally is helping to bring the undesirable alewives under control.) Oil spills, pollution, detergents, even sawdust silt from forest clearing, have all taken terrible tolls of piscine life in many parts of the world. Industrial pollution and overfishing in the Rhine have killed all the salmon in that storied river.

Not all of man's meddling has been so unfortunate. Many food fish have been successfully transplanted to various places around the world. The European brook trout and the American rainbow trout have been highly successful immigrants, fitting smoothly into the local food chains in streams from New Zealand to South Africa, Lake Titicaca notwithstanding. In the last quarter of the 19th century, east coast shad and striped bass were trundled across the United States in tanks on railroad cars, and are now well established along the Pacific seaboard.

Fish farming has become a refined science in such nations as Japan, China, India and the U.S.S.R., which depend for much of their livelihood on the seas and rivers. Artificial breeding has sometimes produced such grotesqueries as the 20,000 two-headed salmon that were the result of an unfortunate experiment in a Dorset, England, hatchery, but it holds the promise of eventually improving the quality and increasing the population of the world's food fish.

For the earth's human population, fulfillment of the promise may be a necessity. As man inexorably diminishes the natural resources of the land, he turns more and more to the seas, rivers, lakes and streams for sustenance. The annual world catch now amounts to a staggering 70 million metric tons of fish, and fishing rights have become matters of international controversy. The cultivation and management of its fishes may one day become the world's last means of sustaining human life.

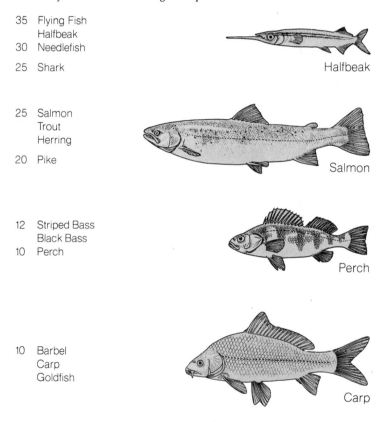

MPH
60	Swordfish
	Sailfish
50	Dolphin
50	Bonito
	Wahoo
	Tuna
40	Mackerel

Wahoo

Despite the fact that water is 800 times denser than air, fish are able to attain speeds that can be favorably compared to those of the fastest land-based, air-breathing animals. The speed a fish may reach relates to size—the fastest fish are among the longest—as well as to shape. The speed of the wahoo, illustrated above, has been estimated at 50 miles per hour. Like all fast swimmers, it has a smooth body that narrows to a slender tail shaft and ends in a firm, deeply forked tail. Its skin is slick and its eyes are flush with its head, providing a minimum of friction. The fish's prominent dorsal fin can be raised for balance or lowered for extra streamlining and speed.

35	Flying Fish
	Halfbeak
30	Needlefish
25	Shark

Halfbeak

25	Salmon
	Trout
	Herring
20	Pike

Salmon

12	Striped Bass
	Black Bass
10	Perch

Perch

10	Barbel
	Carp
	Goldfish

Carp

For their size, the fastest fish of all may be the flying and leaping fish, such as the 12-inch, arrow-shaped halfbeak. But endurance rather than speed is more important to other fish species. The migratory salmon, moving at top speeds of only 25 to 30 miles per hour, can cover up to 50 miles a day in its upstream marathon. Its thicker body and more flexible tail fin suit it for long stretches of swimming in the currents. Active predators such as the bass and the perch reach a relatively sedate 12 miles per hour in pursuit of their prey, while the deep-bodied carp, a shy and cautious omnivore, and its relative the goldfish move only slightly slower.

15

Lakes

The dictionary describes a lake as "a body of water surrounded by land." That terse definition would describe the Caspian Sea or a millpond or a puddle, so limnologists (scientists who specialize in the study of lakes) have added some specifics: Lakes are sizable bodies of standing water with no direct communication to the sea; they must be deep enough so that aquatic plants cannot grow all the way across their bottoms; otherwise they are classified as ponds or lesser bodies of water.

Lakes are formed in the depressions in the earth created by glacial movement, earthquakes, volcanic eruptions or other acts of nature, or by man-made obstructions. Even with those specifications, there are countless different kinds of lakes: freshwater and saltwater, high altitude (windswept Lake Titicaca is two and one third miles high in the Andes) and low (the Dead Sea, a true lake, is 1,302 feet below sea level), lakes with sparkling waters of remarkable clarity and others as dense as pea soup, alkali lakes and bitter lakes and bubbling volcanic lakes, even lakes of black basalt. Lake Superior, the greatest of the Great Lakes, is also the world's largest in area (31,820 square miles), but Lake Baikal, in the heart of Central Asia, is the deepest and the most voluminous, an immense freshwater reservoir caught in a 5,315-foot abyss.

Nearly every lake contains a small, usually well-ordered world of its own. Some lakes are able to support several different species of fish—lake trout in one area, whitefishes and suckers in another, minnows and carps in still another, for example, with each species keeping to its own habitat. Other lakes may have room for only one dominant species: thus, there are walleye lakes, bass lakes, bream lakes. And in each lacustrine society there are predators that perform a function of natural culling that keeps the ecology from disintegrating. Pikes and pickerels, long-bodied killers with glaring eyes and razor teeth, lurk in shoreline weeds and strike passing prey with harpoonlike accuracy. In northern lakes their even larger, more villainous cousin, the muskellunge, performs the same function. The harmless-looking bluegill, a member of the sunfish family, feasts on thousands of eggs of its bass kindred—an act of cannibalism that adult bass also indulge in.

Sometimes the ecological balance of lakes is disturbed by the introduction of undesirable aliens. Parasitic sea lampreys, usually found in rivers (pages 46–47), invaded the Great Lakes through the Welland Canal in the 1920s and annihilated the lake trout; and in the early 1930s a flatworm parasite accidentally entered that superlake, the Aral Sea, on the bodies of transplanted sturgeon, which were introduced by man, and very nearly exterminated the famous native sturgeon. The absence or inefficiency of predators can be even more unsettling to the lacustrine environment. When, for whatever reason, the fishes of a lake produce such a large generation of offspring that it overwhelms the natural predators and the lake cannot sustain it, multitudes of fishes become undernourished, and succeeding generations are likely to be stunted.

Fish often have a natural way of compensating for such imbalances, with fewer fish spawning larger numbers and vice versa. But such natural checks and balances do not always work, especially in man-made reservoirs and impoundments that have been stocked with bass or other game fish, with no thought of natural culling. When such an ecological tragedy occurs, the human solution is often "reclamation"——draining the artificial lake and all its piscine contents and starting all over again, perhaps with a mix of predators and prey that is adequate to maintain the natural balance.

Like the creatures they nurture, lakes are finite, having a beginning, a flourishing middle life, and then dying. Unlike rivers and oceans, every lake begins to die at the moment it is formed, and sooner or later succumbs to the choking forces of encroaching plants and erosion. Some lakes, primarily those in deep basins gouged in granite where vegetation is meager and only the hardiest fish, like certain trout and muskies, can survive, live for many thousands of years. Others, often situated in temperate or tropical regions, live for no more than a generation or two before they become marshes and then rich bottomlands and finally part of the basins of rivers.

The face of the planet is etched with the ghostly outlines of what were once immense living lakes. What is now known as the Qattara Depression in Egypt was in historic times a vast inland sea that nourished a verdant region; it is now part of the Sahara. Lake Agassiz, named for Louis Agassiz, the great 19th century naturalist, once encompassed an area in present-day Canada and Minnesota larger than all of the modern Great Lakes. Lakes that die, though, are replaced by others that are created, either by natural forces or by the hand of man. For lakes and the unique life they sustain are incomparable resources.

Chain pickerel

The pickerel's mottled coloring (left) enables it to hide in the aquatic weeds growing from a lake's sandy bottom. Although they are smaller than the pikes, growing to about three feet in length, pickerels are as hungry as their larger relatives and feed on frogs, minnows and other small fish.

The large, staring orb of the walleye (right) accounts for its name. This important food and game fish is found in large, clear lakes and rivers in North America. Growing to a length of three feet and a weight of over 22 pounds, it is among the largest of the perches.

The fierce-looking northern pike (right) is one of the most widespread species of pikes. A creature of cold waters, it inhabits rivers and lakes throughout northern Asia, Europe and North America up to the Arctic. Northern pikes can grow to be about four feet long and are formidable predators.

Flesh Eaters

Long, slender bodies, dorsal and anal fins located close to the tail, and flattened mouths crammed with sharp, pointed teeth are features that distinguish the fish in the family Esocidae, commonly known as pikes. Also included in the family are the pickerels, smaller replicas of the pikes, and the muskellunge (following pages), the giant of the group. The name pike is also often applied to a number of fishes, such as the walleye (left), which have similar toothy snouts—though the walleye is actually a perch.

Pikes are among the most carnivorous of freshwater fish. Rather than chasing their prey, they resort to the sneak attack. Taking cover in aquatic vegetation, the pike waits motionlessly until a likely target appears. Eyeing its prey with great concentration, the pike lurches forward suddenly, striking with great speed and force. Pikes feed mainly on fish, but some will also attack birds and mammals.

Peak Pike

Whether it is called the muskellunge, lunge, or, as it is often known in Canada, the maskinonge, the musky (the commonest term) is the largest and feistiest member of the pike family. Thirty pounds is common, and individual muskies measuring over five feet and weighing nearly 70 pounds have been reported. Despite its size, the musky is often confused with its close relative, the northern pike. One way to tell them apart is to look for the scales on the cheek: The pike's cheek is entirely covered with scales and the musky's cheek (left) is only partially scaled.

The musky shares the pike family's characteristic anatomy: a long, slender body terminating in dorsal, anal and tail fins that equip it for great acceleration and accuracy in pursuit of a meal. It also exhibits the pikelike penchant for lurking among weeds before striking. The musky inhabits lakes and rivers, where it usually establishes a territory for itself among the aquatic vegetation of a cove or inlet (below). It is from this lair that the musky launches its attack, preying on just about any species of fish it fancies. It has a hearty appetite and the potential for decimating the populations of other fish species. For this reason, smaller bodies of water cannot support large numbers of these predators. This limitation, combined with the fact that the musky is a challenging foe for fishermen as well as a highly edible food fish, has led to a marked decline in its numbers and has limited its present range to the Great Lakes area.

Between meals, the largemouth bass
(left and below) typically lurks in a
shady, weedy area of a lake. However,
when approaching prey it frequently
emerges from the sunless, deeper
water. Special muscles in the lidless
eyes, like those of most fish, adjust the
relationship of the lens to the retina
for close-up or distant viewing.

A largemouth greedily gulps down a
smaller fish (below). A ferocious,
gluttonous predator, the largemouth
will also devour frogs, crayfish, worms,
insects and even fellow bass.

Pugnacious Bass

The largemouth bass (opposite and below), a species widely dispersed throughout the United States and southern Canada, is the largest member of the sunfish family. Its long lower jaw gives a characteristically pugnacious appearance to the fish's mouth, indicative of its short-tempered disposition. The largemouth centers its activities around some stationary object—a submerged tree or stump—that offers a sheltered base of operations. In the spawning season, the male, like all male sunfishes, seeks out shallower water, scrapes a nest in a lake or river bottom with its tail and singles out a female willing to deposit her eggs over the nest. The male often exhibits his usual testiness at this point, nipping angrily at an uncooperative mate and driving her off as soon as the egg laying is completed. He protects the spawn fiercely, fanning them constantly to aerate them, and defends the young fry while they are nourished by the yolk sac until they are ready to fend for themselves.

The burnished glow of the coppernosed bream's forehead (below) accounts for its name. It has been called "one of the fightingest" of the hard-fighting sunfish family. The brightly colored pumpkinseeds (right) have the typical flattened and rounded shape of all sunfishes but are readily identified by the bright red rim of their dark "ear flaps." Because of the pumpkinseed's sharp, spiny fins, other fishes are reluctant to feed on it.

Small Fry

Generally no longer than six to eight inches, the coppernosed bream (above), a local variant of the popular bluegill, and the pumpkinseed (right) are panfish. The term refers to those diminutive species, fished primarily for food, that account for the largest percentage of fish sought by hook-and-line anglers in the United States. Both are members of the sunfish family and share that group's preference for shallow, weedy waters in which to rest and feed on insects, crustaceans and other fish.

The range of the bluegill was once restricted to the Great Lakes area and the Mississippi drainage basin to Florida and Arkansas. But thanks to its successful introduction into farm ponds, it is now found throughout most of the United States. The fact that the bluegill is rarely cannibalistic, however, often leads to a rapid increase in its numbers in such protected ponds and the increased competition for food results in the stunted growth of whole generations of bluegills. The more piscivorous pumpkinseed indiscriminately eats its own kind, as well as other fish, and thereby avoids the consequences of overcrowding.

Desert Relicts

Death Valley was once laced with a network of interconnecting lakes and streams that supported a few varieties of fish, particularly minnows and killifishes. As the area dried following the last ice age, only isolated hot springs and small streams were left in which the fish could live. Unable to adapt to the extremes of these habitats, almost all the minnows perished. But some killifishes survived. The holdouts included four species of the pupfish *Cyprinodon*, such as the Amargosa pupfish (below), found only in Tecopa Hot Springs in California, and one species of killifish, *Empetrichthys* (right), called the Manse Spring poolfish after the Nevada spring where it lives.

Although pupfish have evolved into hardy creatures—some species thrive in waters with temperatures as high as 108° F. and a salinity six times that of seawater—man's destruction of their habitat has resulted in the extermination of several species and the endangerment of others.

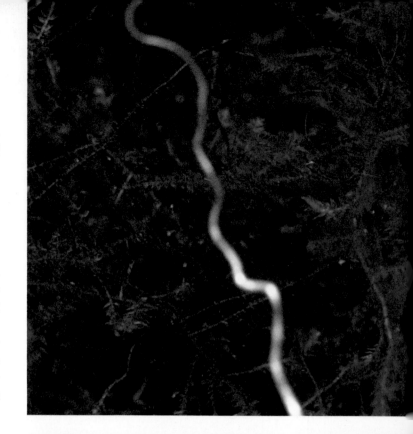

A lone killifish (left) peers through the algae in its tank at the Steinhart Aquarium in San Francisco. Until suitable new waters can be found in which to perpetuate this species—which is threatened in its natural environment—captivity is its only hope for survival.

Immature Amargosa pupfish (below) swim in the waters of their native hot spring. Although pupfish feed primarily on algae, they also consume insects, crustaceans and plankton. Adult males establish small territories, which they defend aggressively against intruders.

Rivers

The rivers, streams, creeks and brooks of the world are a freshwater circulatory system that nourishes the earth, drains continents, provides highways of commerce for mankind, and furnishes hydroelectric energy to light up cities and power industries. The freshwater network also, and lamentably, serves as a natural sewer for the elimination of manufacturing and other human wastes.

The character of rivers and their tributaries differs radically, and even a single riverine system undergoes striking changes between the mountain-bred torrents and streamlets where they begin and the vast mouths where they meet the sea. When they end their vertical descent from the highlands and begin meandering across continental lowlands, many rivers change their courses constantly or slow their flow as they approach the sea. In seasons when the water is low, some southern rivers may stop flowing altogether or even run backward in the teeth of an upstream wind.

All rivers that enter the sea are tidal to some extent; that is, salt water flows into them when the tides are at the flood,

and fresh water surges out to sea with the ebb tide. The Amazon, the mightiest of all rivers, provides a superlative example of tidal movement: The high-tide salt line is 600 miles upstream, and at the ebb, the fresh water flowing into the sea is still discernible 200 miles from the river mouth.

With such an enormous variety of watery habitats, rivers and their feeder streams are the homes of nearly all of the 10,000 species of freshwater fish of the world, and of a host of wanderers like the salmon, shad and eels that inhabit both salt- and freshwater environments at different stages of their lives and use the rivers and streams as busy channels of migration between their two worlds.

The highest, coldest reaches of the riverine world are the natural realm of the trouts, the quintessential freshwater game fishes of North America, Europe and, by extension through artificial stocking, of many streams in Africa, South America, New Zealand and other places as well. Apart from the romance and fiction that surround it in the lore of fishing, the trout is an arctic migratory species that was probably pushed down into more temperate areas by

Brook trout

the movement of glaciers during the ice ages. Trouts are primarily northern fishes that live only in cold, clear waters, mostly mountain rivers and streams in the cooler parts of the temperate zones. A few trouts inhabit lakes, and others, like their brothers the salmon, are anadromous, moving to the sea when they are young and returning as adults to fresh upland waters to spawn.

Trout streams are specialized environments, with intermittant deep pools and shallows, sun-splashed riffles where the fish feed and sandy, slower backwaters where they breed. Brook trout inhabit the colder reaches of streams and cannot tolerate waters warmer than 70°F. The domain of the brown trout, originally a European species, extends to the wider, warmer areas. Cutthroats, natives of mountain streams and rivers of western North America, seek deep pools and overhanging banks. Some trout can survive in the face of battering waterfalls; because of the nutritive qualities, most thrive in streams where the chalk content is high, and the chalk streams of England and Pennsylvania are justly esteemed by trout fishermen and as

carefully maintained as municipal reservoirs.

As the streams widen and empty into rivers and their courses become more horizontal than vertical, other fishes take over. Most of them are also lake fishes: basses, both largemouth and smallmouth, bluegills, crappies, perch, catfish and their cousins, bullheads, and the adaptable carp, an émigré from Eurasia.

Where the rivers run wide, the bigger predatory fish congregate: the pikes and gars, including the sinister-looking alligator gar and the slightly smaller but equally fearsome longnose gar. The world's largest freshwater fish is found, fittingly, in the world's largest river, the Amazon. It is the arapaima, a prehistoric survivor with an ugly depressed snout and both dorsal and anal fins grouped together near its tail. Its dimensions are impressive: Specimens have been reported that weighed 450 pounds and measured 15 feet in length, but they may have been the ones that got away. Reliable statistics report record arapaimas at more than 200 pounds—one of the biggest nonoceanic fishes of all.

29

A Trio of Trout

Cool, clean, fast-flowing, oxygen-rich waters are the habitat of the rainbow trout (right), a prized sport fish of Pacific coast rivers in North America, and other places where it has been stocked. The rainbow of its name derives from the iridescent lateral pink band that runs the length of the trout's body.

The rainbow trout in its oceangoing form is known as the steelhead (opposite, top). Rainbows and steelheads are actually the same fish, but the steelheads migrate to the sea after they are born and remain there for eight months to two years before traveling back, the older ones to spawn in freshwater streams. The steelhead's rainbow stripe becomes indistinct while the fish is in salt water, but reappears when the fish returns to fresh water. Steelheads grow to be larger than those trout remaining in fresh water, regularly reaching weights of six to 10 pounds as compared with the rainbow's average two to eight pounds.

The handsome golden trout (above) is smaller than the rainbow, generally weighing no more than one pound. A denizen of cold mountain streams in the High Sierras, it is never found at altitudes below 8,000 feet. The skin of adult goldens has a burnished glow; as young adults, members of the species retain the vertical marks on their sides that all trout have as parrs, or young fish.

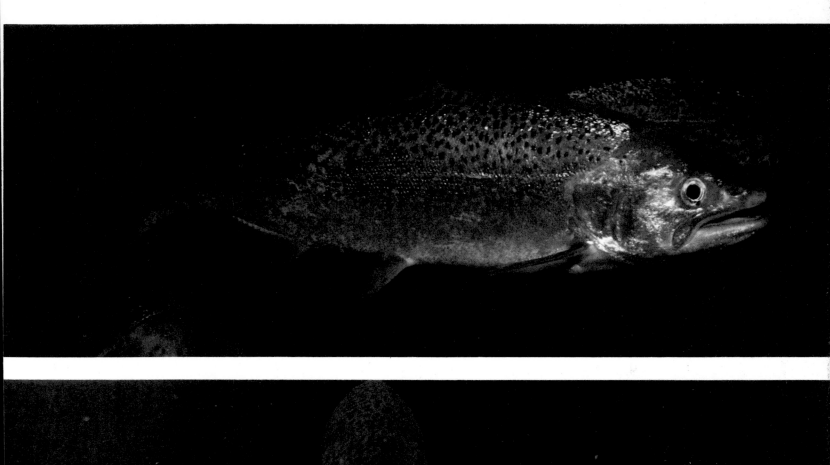

The rest of the world's trout may be taken in summer, to the sound of birds and the pleasant hum of insects, but the steelhead—the big, sea-going rainbow of the Northwest coasts—is winter's child. To know him you must gird as for war and wade the rivers when they are bitter cold—in sleet-filled gloom, or in freezing blue weather when the leafless alders gleam in pale sunlight along the streams, and ice forms in the guides of your rod. To know the steelhead, you should hurt with cold and nurse a little fear of the numbing current which pushes against your waders; it can pull you down and make you gasp and drown you, as steelhead streams methodically drown a few of your fellow fishermen with every passing year.

Excalibur: the Steelhead

by Paul O'Neil

In the following article, Paul O'Neil writes with intimate knowledge of and deep respect for the hardy and handsome steelhead trout and of the unique excitement fishing for this gallant fish brings. Describing himself as a "Northwesterner, trapped in the cities of the East and South," O'Neil has written with extraordinary grace and wit for publications such as Time, Life *and* Sports Illustrated, *in which this article originally appeared in March 1957.*

The steelhead may be pursued in fairer weather, and in easier ways. He runs as far south as the Sacramento River in California. Some of his number run in the early spring, and, in such rivers as the Snake and Oregon's famed Rogue, he runs in the summer, too. But he is a northern fish; when he leaves the sea to spawn, he comes mostly to the rivers of Oregon, Washington, British Columbia, and Alaska, and he migrates chiefly during December, January, and February. The fisherman who has not met him when it is cold has not been properly introduced. Winter sets the stage for him and makes him unique.

There is ominous drama in the very look of a chill, green river on a dark and stormy afternoon, and a man fighting cold and snow to wade it is being properly conditioned for his moment of revelation. For the steelhead is a fish which makes an impact upon the adrenalin-producing glands rather than the intellect. He is always big (six to thirty pounds), and he burns with savage energy from the limitless feed of the ocean he has left behind. He can hurtle into the air a split second after he is hooked, and flash hugely out in the murk, like the sword Excalibur thrust up from

the depths—at once a gleaming prize and a symbol of battle. At that sight, and at the first astounding wrench of the rod, the fisherman is rewarded for his hardihood: he is suddenly warm and reckless, and simultaneously possessed of mindless desperation and rocketing hope.

Men in the grip of this atavistic elation sometimes find themselves doing extraordinary things. A steelhead out in moving water at the end of a six-pound test leader and a nine-pound monofilament line transmits a horrifying sense of power to the rod. Many an otherwise conservative fellow has found himself heedlessly following his fish downstream—laboring wildly along a gravel bar while up to the waist in icy water, body half buoyant, weightless feet feeling desperately for bottom, bucking rod held high and numbed hands working the reel with reverence to get back precious line.

Men have tripped, gone down with a splash, and come up with hardly a change of expression to carry on the struggle; they have run along river banks, hurdling rocks and thrashing out into the water around log jams, in their effort to turn, control, and finally dominate their trout. A lot of them have lost. A few have literally hurled their rods into the stream at the awful second when the line went irrevocably slack. But of course a lot of men—and women, too—have won battles with a big fish in bad water, have guessed when it was time to say, "Now it's you or me," have increased the pressure, controlled the startling submarine disturbance at the end of the line, have endured the trout's last jump and its surface splashing, and have finally reached it—silver, iridescent, and enormous—on shelving gravel or frozen sand and have reached for its gills like a prospector bending at last over the mother lode. And afterwards have relaxed, before an evening fire, in a glow of weariness and euphoria.

Not every struggle with a steelhead is so difficult, for the fish is a creature of moods, and water and weather vary. But the measure of the big trout is his impact upon man, individually and en masse. It is dramatic in the extreme. During the last ten years steelhead fishing has become a near mania in the Northwest. One man in ten in western Washington braves the wintry cold to fish the steelhead streams, and a quarter of a million do so along the West Coast as a whole.

Hundreds of night-shift workers at the Boeing Airplane Company's plants in Seattle and Renton keep rods in their cars and fish on their way home in the morning. Doctors, lawyers, bankers, and engineers fish for steelhead, talk about steelhead and dream about steelhead from November to March. Many a visitor from afar has caught the virus, and many a Northwesterner, trapped in the cities of the East and South, goes on mooning about winter fishing year after year. A lot of people who never fish—but like to eat—applaud the steelhead too. Baked or broiled, he is a delight to the palate; juicy, succulent, similar to salmon in color, taste and texture but with a delicate hint of rainbow trout flavor which is difficult to describe but wonderful to experience.

This furor seems only logical, for the steelhead (*Salmo irideus gairdneri*) which was almost ignored during the Northwest's early decades, is one of the world's toughest and most brilliant game fish and a prince of the beautiful salmonoid family. Pound for pound, he is lustier and more enduring than any of the six strains of Pacific salmon. Unlike them, he does not face inevitable death after spawning—if he can maintain more than sixty per cent of his body weight in migration up a stream, he will get back to the sea, rebuild his strength, grow bigger and return to spawn again.

Exhaustion tests have shown that he can swim for minutes in water fast enough to wash the big king salmon downstream. He is bold: at sea, even as a small fish, he does not school up like Pacific salmon but swims alone. In streams, he is a heavy-water fish, and moves by preference in deep, fast-moving currents. He is hardy: steelhead have come into coastal streams with their body cavities ripped open by sharks and have still hit a lure and have fought gallantly. He is an amazing jumper. Pacific salmon have never surmounted Shipherd's Falls, a roaring, sixty-foot cataract in Washington's Wind River (although they now negotiate it by fish ladder), but the steelhead is able to pick his way up by leaping from one small pocket of water, four, five, or six feet to the next, often jumping at odd angles to hit the targets he must sense but cannot possibly see as he launches himself.

Brazilian Originals

In the jungles of Brazil two primitive fish species—the giant arapaima (above and opposite, top) and the arawana (opposite, bottom)—thrive in the murky waters of the Amazon River basin. The arapaima is widely considered to be the largest fish inhabiting an exclusively freshwater habitat, and many individuals grow to a length of seven to eight feet and weigh 200 pounds. For all this bulk, arapaimas are anything but ungainly, manipulating their heavy bodies easily through the water.

The silt-choked Amazonian waters are often low in oxygen content, and the arapaima has evolved a means of breathing air at the surface to supplement the intake of oxygen from the river. Its swim bladder functions as a lung—connected to the throat by a duct—and is richly supplied with blood vessels that assimilate the atmospheric oxygen. During the breeding season arapaimas seek out clearer, shallower areas with sandy soil, where they hollow out nests with their fins. The nests may be 20 inches in diameter and six inches deep. The male, which performs a key role in the lives of the young, has been observed to carry eggs in his mouth—perhaps to move them away from danger. At other times the young, apparently attracted by a glandular secretion, collect near the male's head, forming a family unit.

The delicately colored, two-foot-long arawana inhabits the same waters as its relative and is its favorite food.

The bulging eyes of the giant arapaima (above and right, top) are adapted to spotting prey in its murky habitat. The dorsal and anal fins are positioned so far back on its elongated body that they appear to be connected with the small tail fin.

The lower jaw of the arawana (right) slopes at a sharp angle to meet the upper one, and two fleshy barbels protrude from the tip of the lower jaw. The arawana was photographed from below, in a controlled situation, and reflected light produces an optical illusion—a distorted double image.

The selective breeding of ornamental goldfish has long been an exotic industry in Japan, where a single prize specimen can command almost $17,000. The magnificent golden carps above, looking as though they had been fashioned by some oriental Cellini, amiably share their pool with a smaller redheaded breed. Another species of golden carp (right) is bred for its vivid orange and black splotches.

In their natural state, carps are bronze, heavy-bodied fish with barbel feelers to locate food and up to three rows of grinding teeth located in their throats. They can tolerate murky, stagnant pools where oxygen is low and food plentiful, living and foraging for young plants on the bottom. Many species are fully scaled, but the mirror carp at left is only partly scaled.

Carps of Gold

Each May 5, Japan celebrates a national holiday, Boys' Day, when every home where there is a male child displays banners shaped and painted to look like carps. The symbolic fish represents the courage and fortitude of its upstream struggles, an example for every Japanese boy to follow. The carp is esteemed throughout Asia and Europe, more as a dietary staple than an example of bravery—with an annual world catch of 200,000 tons, carps rank among the most important of food fish—and as an ancient and fascinating ornamental fish. In the United States and other temperate parts of the world where it has been widely introduced, the carp is regarded rather skeptically as a sometime destroyer of native fishes and a nuisance, but it still rouses grudging admiration as one of the world's hardiest and most intelligent fishes.

The carp family, which includes minnows, shiners, goldfishes, chubs and daces, has more species than any other fish family. Species of carp and goldfish (left and below), have been bred as domestic aquarium and pond fishes in China and Japan for 1,000 years or more. In China alone there are more than 120 recognized forms of goldfishes. The Japanese breed their goldfishes to resemble swimming flowers.

A Fishy Affair

by Anton Chekhov

Son of a grocer, grandson of a serf, Anton Chekhov began his illustrious literary career writing broad, comic pieces under a pseudonym in order to support himself and his family while he attended medical school. In A Fishy Tale, reprinted below, Chekhov reveals his personal theory about the mysterious origins of the pessimism supposedly inherent in all poets.

Strange as it may sound, the only carp in the pond near General Pantalykin's cottage fell head over heels in love with a holiday visitor, Sonya Mamochkin. But is that really so very remarkable? Lermontov's Demon fell in love with Tamara, after all, and the swan loved Leda. And don't clerks occasionally fall for the boss's daughter? Sonya Mamochkin came for a bathe with her aunt each morning and the lovesick carp swam near the pond edge watching her. Close proximity to the foundry of Krandel and Sons had turned the water brown ages ago, yet the carp could see everything. He saw white clouds and birds soaring through the azure sky, he saw bathing beauties undressing, he saw peeping toms watching them from bushes on the bank and he saw a fat old woman sitting on a rock

Sonya Mamochkin

complacently stroking herself for five minutes before going in the water.

'Why am I such a great fat cow?' she said. 'Oh, I do look awful!'

Doffing her ethereal garments, Sonya dived into the water with a shriek, swam about, braced herself against the cold—and there, sure enough, was the carp. He swam up to her and began avidly kissing her feet, shoulders, neck.

Cyprinus carpio

Their dip over, the girls went home for tea and buns while the solitary carp swam round the enormous pond.

'There can be no question of reciprocity, of course,' he thought. 'As if a beautiful girl like that would fall in love with a carp like me! No, no, a thousand times no! So don't indulge in such fancies, O wretched fish! You have only one course left: death. But what death? This pond lacks revolvers and phosphorous matches. There is only one possible death for us carp: a pike's jaws. But where can I find a pike? There was a pike in this pond once, but even it died of boredom. Oh, I am so miserable!'

Brooding on death, the young pessimist buried himself in mud and wrote a diary.

Late one afternoon Sonya and her aunt were sitting at the edge of the pond fishing. The carp swam near the floats, feasting his eyes on his beloved. Suddenly an idea flashed through his head.

'I shall die by her hand,' thought he with a gay flip of the fins. 'How marvellous, how sweet a death!'

Resolute yet blenching slightly, he swam up to Sonya's hook and took it in his mouth.

'Sonya, you have a bite!' shrieked Aunty. 'You've caught something, my dear!'

'Oh, Oh!'

Sonya jumped up and tugged with all her might. Something golden flashed in the air and flopped on the water, making ripples.

'It got away!' both women shouted, turning pale. 'It got away! Oh, my dear!'

They looked at the hook and saw a fish's lower lip on it.

'Oh, you shouldn't have pulled so hard, dear,' said Aunty. 'Now that good fish has no lip.'

After snatching himself off the hook our hero was flabbergasted and it was some time before he realized what was happening to him. Then he came to.

'To live again!' groaned he. 'Oh, mockery of fate!'

But noticing that he was minus a lower jaw, the carp blenched and uttered a wild laugh. He had gone mad.

Deranged Carp

It may seem odd, I fear, that I should wish to detain the serious reader's attention with the fate of so insignificant and dull a creature as a carp. What is so odd about that, though? After all, ladies in literary magazines describe utterly futile tiddlers and snails. And I am imitating those ladies. Perhaps I may even *be* a lady and am just hiding behind a man's pseudonym.

So our carp went mad. That unhappy fish is still alive. Most carps like to be served fried with sour cream, but my hero would settle for any death now. Sonya Mamochkin has married a man who keeps a chemist's shop and Aunty has gone to her married sister's in Lipetsk, though there is nothing odd in that because the married sister has six children and they all adore their aunt.

Ivan, the Writer of Verse

But let us continue. Engineer Krysin is director of the foundry of Krandel and Sons. He has a nephew Ivan, well known as a writer of verse which he eagerly publishes in all the magazines and papers. Passing the pond one hot noontide, our young poet conceived the notion of taking a dip, removed his clothes and entered the pond. The mad carp took him for Sonya Mamochkin, swam up and tenderly kissed his back. That kiss had most fatal consequences: the carp infected our poet with pessimism. Suspecting nothing, the poet climbed out of the water and went home, uttering wild guffaws. Several days later he went to St. Petersburg. Having visited some editorial offices there, he infected all the poets with pessimism, from which time onwards our poets have been writing gloomy, melancholy verse.

Catfish Row

Catfishes are found throughout most of the world—generally in freshwater rivers and swamps, and also in the oceans. Many catfishes are an excellent food source, and there are farms where they are bred for the market. Breeding is easy—catfishes are very hardy and can exist in varieties of water temperature and even in polluted water.

Most catfishes are virtually scaleless (though some have armorlike plating) and are identifiable by the catlike whiskers, the feelers called barbels, that give them their name. The barbels have taste buds that help the fish to search for food. Cats use their barbels to probe the murky water where their weak eyes cannot penetrate.

Among the 2,000 species of catfishes, spawning habits vary greatly. Some freshwater catfishes are capable of laying thousands of eggs at a time. Some of these species simply spray their eggs into shallow depressions, while others build nests on the undersides of vegetation that lies on the water's surface. Still another type may work for two to three days in order to excavate a nest in the muddy bottom. In some marine species, the male carries up to 55 of the marble-size eggs in his mouth for the entire month they take to hatch, and holds the live babies in there off and on for another two weeks. During the entire time he eats nothing at all.

The long flattened head of a South American catfish (above) has earned it the name of "shovelnose." A dweller in fast-flowing waters, this catfish has a mouth located far behind its barbels, which are often as long as its body.

An African catfish (right) is a member of the family Clariedae, distinguished by long and spineless dorsal and anal fins. Equipped with a lunglike cavity as well as gills, it can survive out of water for extended periods.

The barbels of a lion-headed catfish (left) are hardly visible beside the branchlike growth on its head. This inhabitant of India and Indonesia is probably the most lethargic of all catfishes. It will only move from the bottom to feed.

In the mid-1960s the walking catfish (right) was imported as an aquarium curiosity to Florida from Southeast Asia and somehow managed to escape to the wild. It is quite capable of surviving out of the water for 12 hours. The milky-gray albino variety has traveled overland throughout southern Florida, where it menaces native fishes, snails and crustaceans and is considered a serious threat to the ecosystem.

A slender channel catfish (right) gulps down a small fish. Channel catfish, often confused with the classic American cats that Huckleberry Finn fished for, will eat anything digestible, alive or dead. When hunting food they trail their barbels across the mud bottom.

A parasitic lamprey (left) displays its rounded, funnel-like mouth, which it uses to cling to its victims by suction. Once attached, the lamprey scrapes and pierces the host's flesh with its rasping tongue. Lampreys and the equally ancient hagfishes are the only living fishes without jaws.

Lampreys prey on a carp (below). Once a lamprey attaches itself to a fish the victim may be unable to escape from the bloodsucking parasite and dies from loss of blood or flesh. Sometimes three or four lampreys attack the same fish and "ride" their prey until it dies.

Bloodsuckers of the Sea

The 14 species of lampreys that live in the rivers and seas of North America can be divided into two groups: parasitic and nonparasitic. Both types can use their suction-cuplike mouths to adhere to rocks and prevent themselves from drifting downstream.

The lamprey also uses its special mouth to move stones while preparing a nest—a shallow, pebble-lined trough where the female lamprey lays and the male fertilizes the tiny eggs, and then die. Newly hatched lampreys look so different from adults that they have their own name, "prides." The blind worm-shaped larvae float downstream and bury themselves in mud, exposing only their gaping toothless mouths to strain algae from the water. Several years later—an extraordinarily long period of infantile limbo for a fish—they suddenly metamorphose into adults,

with eyes and a sucking, toothed mouth. The sea lamprey migrates to salt water, where it spends one to nearly two years as a lethal parasite, attached to the bodies of other fishes, only returning upriver to spawn and die. The nonparasitic lamprey never leaves fresh water; some migrate upstream after metamorphosis, and spawn and die within a very short time.

Among the most primitive fishes, lampreys are not equipped with normal gills. Instead they both inhale and expel water through seven pairs of gill openings on the sides of their heads (opposite). They were considered a delicacy in medieval Europe—where they once thrived—and one English monarch, Henry I, is said to have died from eating too many of them. Today, however, their popularity as a food fish has waned considerably.

A gar (right) seizes a victim after lunging from its weedy cover. First it had positioned itself carefully so that its prey was to one side of its jaws. Then it snapped its head over and made the capture.

The schooling gars below are swimming close to the surface. Young gars are often mistaken for small twigs drifting on top of the water.

Freshwater "Shark"

With its "armor" of patterned scales, its needle-sharp teeth, and its narrow, streamlined body that is well adapted for nimble, speedy maneuvering, the gar (above) is a fearsome predator. The large, dark spots on its head, snout and body serve the gar as effective camouflage, especially when it basks motionlessly, buoyed close to the water's surface by a complex swim bladder that serves the fish as an additional respiratory organ. Its protective scales do not overlap but fit together snugly and smoothly, a pattern that is typical of the gar family and that is an oddity in the modern fish world.

The longnose is the most widely distributed species, with a protruding elongated snout and long, slim body. Not restricted to quiet backwaters, it feeds in the moderately swift-moving mainstream. The most spectacular species is the alligator gar, which has been measured at 10 feet and weighed at 302 pounds. Called by some the "shark of freshwater fish," the gar has a double row of sharp teeth on each side of its upper jaw, and preys on insect larvae, crayfish and small forage fish such as the threadfin shad and golden shiner. Like all gars, it snatches victims with an abrupt, sideways jerk of its head.

50

The sturgeon (left) prefers a lake or river bed of sand or gravel that allows clear, unobstructed access to its bottom-dwelling food supply—snails, crayfish and insect larvae.

Dispensers of Luxury

The sturgeon family includes some of the world's largest freshwater fishes, notably the beluga sturgeon (opposite, bottom), which has weighed in on one occasion at one ton and with a length of 13 feet. From its eggs comes the world-renowned beluga caviar. The demand for the luxury food is so great that production is now carefully controlled by protective conservation measures and artificial breeding in the Soviet Union and Iran. The Russian beluga is anadromous, moving from its Caspian and Black Sea habitats to freshwater spawning grounds and choosing a convenient hole where the female deposits her millions of pearly gray eggs.

Some 20 species of sturgeon are found in temperate waters in the Northern Hemisphere, where they have lived for 65 million years. The sturgeon grows at a slow rate, reaching sexual maturity after 12 to 20 years. This is one explanation for the scarcity of caviar, since very few sturgeons manage to reach an age when they have the opportunity to ensure the species' survival by spawning.

The beluga sturgeon at left exhibits a toothless mouth under a pointed snout, from which droop four tactile whiskers that supplement the fish's weak eyesight in navigating and locating prey. When the fish senses food, the mouth drops open and siphons it in. The taste buds are located on the outside of the mouth.

Tagging studies of the migratory patterns of the Columbia River sturgeon (right) show that in winter the immature fish swims upstream, remaining until early spring, then starts downstream again—probably in search of food—and travels a daily maximum of five miles.

The thin, flat snout of the paddlefish (right) is one third the length of its body and has sensory receptors, possibly for detecting the presence of plankton in the water. A male bowfin (below) can be easily recognized by the black spot at the base of its caudal fin. Bowfins often undulate only their dorsal fin when swimming slowly.

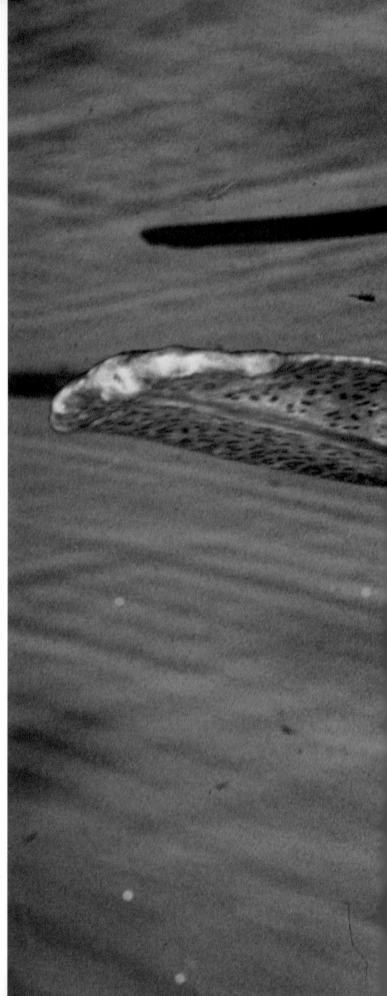

Elders of the River

The bowfin, or freshwater dogfish (above), and the improbable-looking paddlefish (right) are unrelated relics of two ancient groups of ray-finned bony fishes—a lineage that is attested to by their primitive tails (see chart, pages 12–13). Both are natives of the rivers of the Mississippi-Missouri drainage basin (another related paddlefish is found in China, but the bowfin is exclusively a North American fish).

A voracious predator, the bowfin feeds on other fishes, principally game fishes like the largemouth bass, and it therefore arouses ambiguous feelings among fishermen: Some deplore it for its depredations of game fish populations; others, recognizing its prowess as a feisty fighter, regard it as a game fish itself.

The paddlefish poses no such problems for the fishing fraternity: It feeds only on minute plankton that inhabit the waters of its habitat. Swimming along the river, it drops its great jaw like a steam shovel, scooping up food and muck together and separating the nutrients with its fine gill rakers. Paddlefish are valued for their fine flesh and their eggs, which are sold as a type of caviar. Extensive dam building and power projects, however, have cut them off from spawning sites and they are now rare.

Spawning

The rite of reproduction in fishes usually involves nothing more complicated than a male releasing his sperm, or milt, over the newly laid eggs of a female to fertilize them. But the variations on that act—and the hardships some fishes undergo to accomplish it—are nearly incredible.

Some fishes are live-bearers. One hybrid molly copulates with random males of certain other similar species without any hybridization occurring, and brings forth only females, which are exact replicas of their mothers. Among the cichlids are oral brooders: The female *Tilapia mossambica*, for instance, scoops up her eggs into her mouth after a male has fertilized them and spits them out as fully formed baby fish after 10 to 12 days incubation.

Most fish are egg layers that spawn in the water, producing thousands, even millions of eggs to ensure the continuation of their species. Some oceanic fishes, such as cods, swarm together in immense schools during the spawning season, releasing millions of eggs and clouds of milt indiscriminately. The eggs float on the surface of the sea until they hatch, in as little as 10 days. Other saltwater fish, such as grunions and capelins, a species of smelt, head instinctively for the shore at spawning time. Grunions writhe together on the beach in a strange mating dance until the female deposits her eggs three inches under the sand, where they are fertilized and lie for two weeks, until the next spring tide washes the hatching young into the sea.

Many freshwater fish lay their eggs in nests that they scoop with their tails from the graveled or sandy bottoms of lakes or streams, or laboriously dredge, pebble by pebble, with their mouths. Sometimes the eggs lie exposed, guarded by one or both parents until they hatch; other clutches are covered by protective layers of pebbles, which are loosely packed so that the incubating eggs receive enough oxygen. Spawning in fresh water usually involves some migration, which may be a trip of only a few yards upstream or a journey of a hundred miles or more. Among the long-distance swimmers the undoubted champions are the anadromous fishes, those dual-life species that originate in fresh water, live out most of their lives in the sea, and are drawn by unknown impulses to return to their native streams to spawn and, in some species, to die. The steelhead trout, the shad, the striped bass and some sturgeons are all anadromous spawners, but the most famous, the fish that makes the most incredible journeys to reproduce itself, is undoubtedly the salmon.

Salmon fall into two categories: the single Atlantic species and six species that frequent both shores of the Pacific—the huge Chinook, the smaller silver, or coho, the sockeye (opposite), chum, pink and the cherry, an Asiatic species. The Atlantic salmon is found from the Arctic Circle to Cape Cod in the New World and from the Arctic Circle to the Bay of Biscay in Europe. The Pacific varieties are distributed along both the east and west coasts of that ocean, from Japan to California and north to Alaska. Every salmon begins life as a one-fourth-inch globe about the size of a pea buried in the gravelly bed of a swift-running stream. After hatching, the tiny fish undergoes several stages of development, most with old Anglo-Saxon names: alevin, (hatchlings), fry (able to feed themselves), parr (about two inches long), smolts (four to eight inches long and ready to head for the ocean), grilse (16 inches long) and kelt (the stage after a first spawning).

Once they are at sea, the adult salmon may remain for only one year or as long as five and may travel less than a few thousand miles from the mouth of their native river or roam the high seas for 10,000 miles. The return trip upstream to spawn is highly dramatic. Salmon that are homeward bound run rapids, ascend waterfalls, circumvent dams, and even slither across rocks to reach the particular stream where they were born, there to spawn and usually to die.

The saga of the catadromous fishes, especially the common eels, is more mysterious. Spending their adult lives in streams of North America and Europe, and of Asia and Australia, all eels return to the sea where they were born, to spawn and die. For centuries, their reproduction was a mystery. Aristotle declared that eels were sexless, cast up by the entrails of the earth. Only in the 1920s was it finally determined that all Atlantic eels are born in the Sargasso Sea, a weed-choked mid-ocean navigational landmark 1,000 miles from the nearest American river mouth and three or four times as far from any European stream.

After an infancy in the Sargasso's weeds, millions of young larvae set forth in armadas on a northward course. Somewhere near the latitude of Bermuda they separate into two groups, with the American species heading west to their ancestral streams and the others turning east toward Europe. How and why they manage this astonishing maneuver is as much a puzzle as their origins were in Aristotle's time, some 2,000 years ago.

Spawning salmon

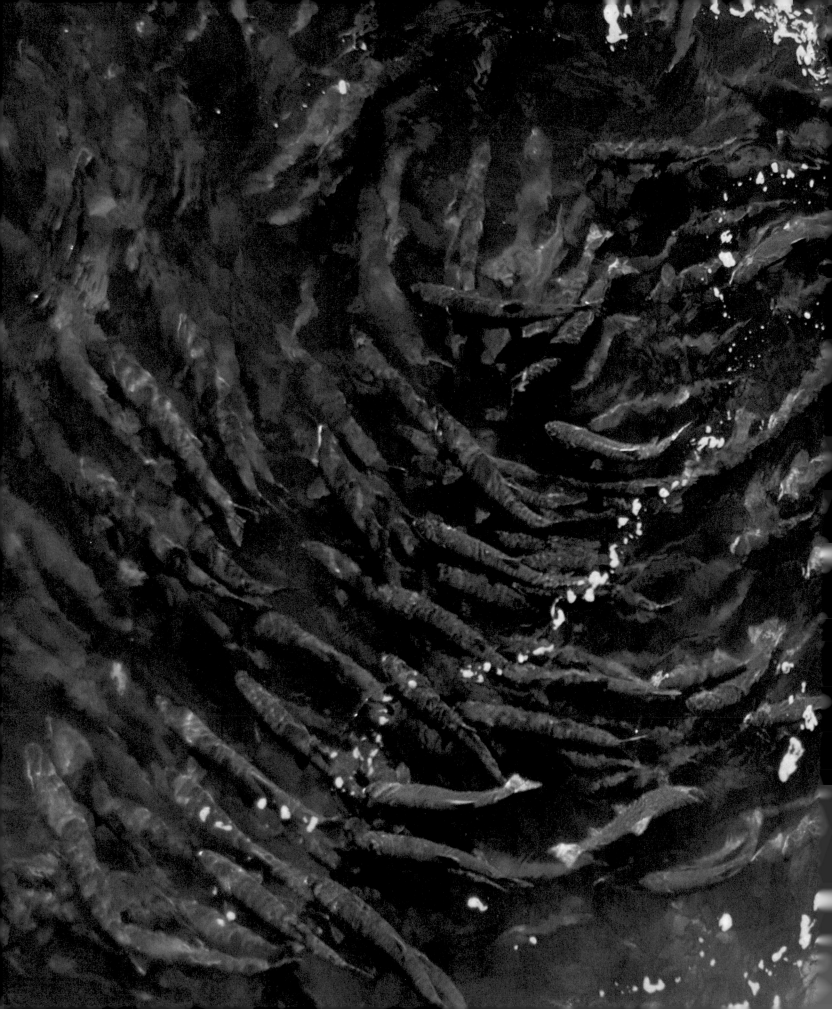

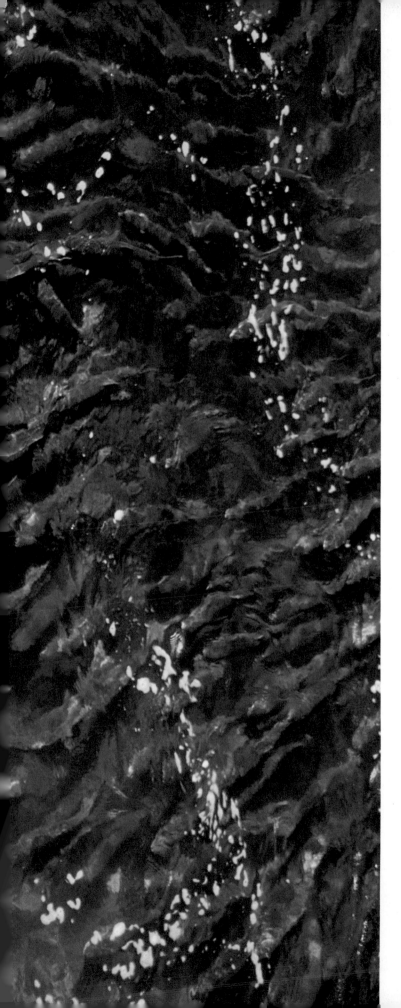

Incredible Journey

The mass of sockeye salmon shown on these pages is gathering in the Adams River in British Columbia before beginning its bruising, demanding, 300-mile upstream journey—each individual determinedly, instinctively, homing in on its own particular spawning ground where its journey began as much as four years earlier.

Like all salmons, the sockeye, or red, salmon lives only in cold, oxygen-rich Northern Hemisphere waters. The origins of its dual marine and freshwater existence are unclear, but scientists speculate that freshwater salmons originally inhabited arctic lakes and streams, and that with the coming of the ice ages about a million years ago, a shortage of food in these former freshwater regions forced them to venture into the sea in search of sustenance.

In the course of its oceanic wanderings the sockeye's body weight increases to an average of five or six pounds and may even reach 15 pounds. Dispersing over thousands of miles of Pacific Ocean, even traveling as far north as the Bering Sea, the sockeyes consume everything from zooplankton to crustaceans. But when the instinct to spawn asserts itself after two or three years at sea, the sockeyes return to the same fresh water where they were hatched.

57

As sockeyes move toward their spawning grounds (left) their silvery seagoing coloration changes radically. The fiery, lively, crimson-colored body of its final freshwater phase contrasts vividly with the cool olive green of the head.

During the 15-day trip in the shallow waters (right) the male's jaw elongates, the hook at the tip of the lower jaw grows rapidly and a pronounced hump develops on the back. The larger female's body is heavy with roe.

Sockeyes leap up a waterfall, swimming against the current (below). Scientists now speculate that salmon, nearing the end of their marine phase, use some navigational technique to chart a return course. Experiments show that an olfactory sense takes over when sockeyes are within smelling distance of their starting point.

During the courtship ritual that precedes spawning, the male sockeye (right) swims back and forth over the female as she rests near the bottom, touching her dorsal fin and nudging her with his snout.

While the female prepares the redd, the male (above) defends the territory from intruders and possible rivals for the female's attentions.

Moments after the bright-pink eggs are laid and fertilized, the female (right) turns her head upstream and churns gravel with her battered tail to cover the eggs—loosely, so that their oxygen supply is not cut off.

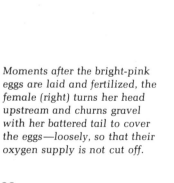

Culmination

Spawning, the culmination of the struggle, takes place not in some still backwater, but in the swift-running river current. First, the female prepares the redd, or nest, clearing away stones with her tail, digging down to the gravel bed of the stream. She slips over on her side at an angle of 45 degrees to the current, head pointed upstream. This takes advantage of the moving current, which engulfs and sweeps away any debris, leaving a clean, smooth incubation bed that will eventually be about twice as long as the industrious nester herself.

Larger, immovable stones will provide convenient crannies to anchor the eggs securely and prevent them from being swept downstream. When the redd is finished, the female hovers over the nest while the male aligns his body with hers, and the eggs are laid and the milt washed over them simultaneously. The sperm enters the egg through a tiny pore called the micropyle.

The Cycle's End

Unlike the Atlantic salmon, which returns to the sea after spawning, sometimes repeating the reproductive cycle three or four times during its life, the Pacific salmon invariably dies soon after the eggs have been laid. A few days after the spawning ritual is finished, the males become listless, drifting helplessly with the current and quickly losing their brilliant color (left).

The decaying carcasses remaining in the river (below) provide nourishment for bears, birds and other scavengers foraging on the banks. When the organic elements are released into the water with the spring thaw, they nourish the plankton that will eventually be consumed by the newly hatched salmon.

Thus the cycle ends in death for the elder sockeyes, often mere yards from the sites where they originally hatched several years earlier.

The sight of dead and dying sockeyes at left is a pitiful aftermath of the spectacle of the colorful, gallant upstream migration. The played-out fish can barely drift about in the current; their eyes are dim and many have only enough strength to lie on the riverbed waiting to die.

63

The New Generation

Until the coming of spring, the tiny, bright-pink salmon eggs lie buried in the deep gravel of the chilly stream, often securely tucked between larger rocks that escaped the sweeping motions of the mother's tail. When the hatchlings, or alevins, first emerge, a nourishing yolk sac is attached to their bellies; until it is absorbed the alevins are unable to eat and they remain near the gravelly streambed. After several weeks as fry, they are ready to forage for food.

When the sockeyes have reached the fingerling stage and are two inches long, they are carried out of the swiftly moving current into quieter, deeper river waters or into a lake. There, dark body markings provide excellent and indispensable camouflage. The lake serves as a sort of nursery until the young sockeyes reach the smolt stage and their bodies begin to undergo the physiological changes necessary for adaptation from a freshwater to a marine existence. For their ocean sojourn, the salmon develop a bright-silver coloration, while their gill and kidney systems undergo adaptations that will fit them for their peregrinations.

Two million sockeye eggs may produce only 19,000 smolts (right). This is the stage at which the small salmon head downstream and eventually out to sea.

The incubating sockeyes (left) have developed eyes and are equipped with yolk sacs that provide nourishment until they hatch and are capable of searching out food for themselves.

The fry (left) is about one inch long. While in this vulnerable stage it hovers close to the rocky streambed to avoid bright light and such predators as the cutthroat trout, birds and snakes.

Brook Babies

Found in most of the United States and a favorite of anglers, the brook trout is like its close cousin the salmon, a dweller in cool, clean, fast-flowing brooks and mountain streams as well as lakes. The brook trout begins to spawn at the end of fall or early winter. Unlike the salmon, this trout is essentially nonmigratory, traveling relatively short distances in search of an appropriate gravelly spot upstream in which to build its nest and lay its eggs.

Once at the spawning site, the trouts pair off. As the female excavates the nest—a roundish depression that can be from one to two feet in diameter and from two to 10 inches deep, depending on the size of the fish—the male stands guard, fending off all intruders. The couple release their roe and milt almost simultaneously, for the milt is fertile for only a few moments. The female immediately covers them with a thin blanket of gravel to protect them from egg-eating predators and from being washed away during the three-week to three-month gestation period.

A female brook trout deposits her eggs in the stone-studded bottom of a Colorado stream (left). The number of eggs a female produces is determined by her size. An eight-inch fish may lay only 300 eggs, while the nest of a 12-inch trout may contain one thousand eggs.

The spermatozoa from a male brook trout washes over eggs just laid by his mate (right). Newly hatched larval trout have protruding abdomens to encase the yolk sacs on which they feed during their first few weeks of life.

A crush of brook trout swims through a narrow pass in a Colorado stream (below) on their way to spawn. Trout are not sociable fish and once they reach a wider part of the waterway they will break up into mating pairs.

A slithering, silvery mass of grunions (below) is washed onto the sands of a California beach. Here, in a matter of 20 to 30 seconds, their eggs will be laid, fertilized and buried, safe from the predations of sea-dwelling enemies.

With a stirring motion of her tail, a female grunion (right) buries herself almost vertically in the sand; then, arching her body from side to side, she lays her eggs. Males swirl around her, depositing their milt over the eggs as they are released.

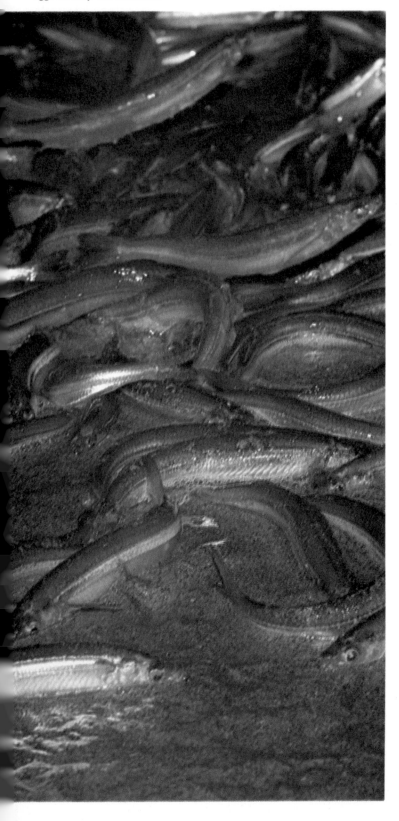

Moonstruck

For centuries the moon has been a universal symbol of romantic love. But for the grunion, a silvery little smeltlike fish from southern California, the glowing orb is an indispensable guide to mating and procreation. Unlike most other fishes, the grunion comes up on land to spawn; it is drawn there by high tides occurring at certain phases of the moon, which cast them by the thousands on the moist sands of California beaches. Once on shore, the female grunion immediately burrows into the sand and deposits her eggs a few inches below the surface. The males thereupon fertilize the eggs and, as the surf covers them with an extra layer of sand, the adults return to the sea. Once all the adults have left, the beach bears no trace of their presence. But inches beneath the sand the eggs are developing, a process that takes about 10 days. Thus, when the next spring tide begins to pound the sand, the eggs are ready to hatch. Successive waves erode their sandy cover and the young grunions are carried out to sea.

A male Haplochromis burtoni displays his brightly marked anal fins to his prospective mate (left). He swims over a stone that he has cleaned of sand, where the female will lay her eggs.

As her mate hovers nearby, a female mouth brooder picks up her newly laid eggs (left). The eggs, which number from 30 to 80, are kept in an extended area of the female's throat sac until ready to hatch.

A male mouth brooder displays his anal fin in front of his mate's face (left). As the female approaches to inspect his egglike markings, the male will release milt to fertilize the eggs.

Mouth Brooders

The cichlids, a family of the order Perciformes, are a group of primarily freshwater tropical fish that have become popular among aquarium owners, despite their cannibalistic habits and often unsociable dispositions in captivity. The attraction for home fish fanciers is the cichlids' fascinating method of reproduction. Although some cichlids procreate through normal spawning, many, such as the colorful African species seen on these pages, *Haplochromis burtoni*, engage in what is called mouth brooding.

Mating begins conventionally enough, with a male and a female pairing off. The pair first make a nest in a slight depression in the sand or on the surface of some smooth, hard object like a stone. When the receptacle is prepared the female lays her mustard-seed-size eggs and im-

mediately scoops them up in her mouth. She is then enticed by the swirling movements of the male's feathery anal fins, which are decorated with brilliant red-orange markings called egg spots. Perhaps under the impression that they are some eggs she has missed, the female tries to gobble them up too. Instead, the male releases his sperm into her mouth, thereby fertilizing the eggs.

Incubation lasts 10 to 14 days. The female regularly shifts the eggs around in her mouth during this time, ensuring adequate aeration. Once they hatch, the young leave their mother's mouth but stay close by her (below) so if danger threatens, they have a handy refuge in their mother's open mouth. This protective custody lasts only a week, until the fry are large enough to go off on their own.

In her books Silent Spring, The Sea Around Us *and* The Edge of the Sea *Rachel Carson brings a wealth of scientific knowledge and a gift for rich, poetic description to her subjects, marine biology and ecology. The excerpt below, taken from* Under the Sea Wind, *describes the exhilarating but perilous journey of an eel, Anguilla, as she returns to her spawning ground.*

Under the Sea Wind

by Rachel Carson

As the river widened and deepened, a strange taste came into the water. It was a slightly bitter taste, and at certain hours of the day and night it grew stronger in the water that the eels drew into their mouths and passed over their gills. With the bitter taste came unfamiliar movements of the water—a period of pressure against the downflow of the river currents followed by slow release and then swift acceleration of the current. Now groups of slender posts stood at intervals in the river, marking out funnel shapes from which straight rows of posts ran slanting toward the shore. Blackened netting, coated with slimy algae, was run from post to post and showed several feet above the water. Gulls were often sitting on the pound nets, waiting for men to come and fish the nets so that they could pick up any fish that might be thrown away or lost. The posts were coated with barnacles and with small oysters, for now there was enough salt in the water for these shellfish to grow.

Sometimes the sandspits of the river were dotted with small shore birds standing at rest or probing at the water's edge for snails, small shrimps, worms, or other food. The shore birds were of the sea's edge, and their presence in numbers hinted of the nearness of the sea.

The strange, bitter taste grew in the water and the pulse of the tides beat stronger. On one of the ebb tides a group of small eels—none more than two feet long—came out of a brackish-water marsh and joined the migrants from the hill streams. They were males, who had never ascended the rivers but had remained within the zone of tides and brackish water.

In all of the migrants striking changes in appearance were taking place. Gradually the river garb of olive brown was changing to a glistening black, with underparts of silver. These were the colors worn only by mature eels about to undertake a far sea journey. Their bodies were firm and rounded with fat—stored energy that would be needed before the journey's end. Already in many of the migrants the snouts were becoming higher and more compressed, as though from some sharpening of the sense of smell. Their eyes were enlarged to twice their normal size, perhaps in preparation for a descent along darkening sea lanes. . . .

The eels spent a week descending the bay, hurrying through water of increasing saltiness. The currents moved with a rhythm that was of neither river nor sea, being governed by eddies at the mouths of the many rivers that emptied into the bay and by holes in the muddy bottom thirty or forty feet beneath. The ebb tides ran stronger than the floods, because the strong outflow of the rivers resisted the press of water from the sea.

At last Anguilla neared the mouth of the bay. With her were thousands of eels, come down, like the water that brought them, from all the hills and uplands of thousands of square miles, from every stream and river that drained away to the sea by the bay. The eels followed a deep channel that hugged the eastern shore of the bay and came to where the land passed into a great salt marsh. Beyond the marsh, and between it and the sea, was a vast shallow

arm of the bay, studded with islands of green marsh grass. The eels gathered in the marsh, waiting for the moment when they should pass to the sea.

The next night a strong southeast wind blew in from the sea, and when the tide began to rise the wind was behind the water, pushing it into the bay and out into the marshes. That night the bitterness of brine was tasted by fish, birds, crabs, shellfish, and all the other water creatures of the marsh. The eels lay deep under water, savoring the salt that grew stronger hour by hour as the wind-driven wall of sea water advanced into the bay. The salt was of the sea. The eels were ready for the sea—for the deep sea and all it held for them. Their years of river life were ended.

The wind was stronger than the forces of moon and sun, and, when the tide turned an hour after midnight, the salt water continued to pile up in the marsh, being blown upstream in a deep surface layer while the underlying water ebbed to the sea.

Soon after the tide turn, the seaward movement of the eels began. In the large and strange rhythms of a great water which each had known in the beginning of life, but each had long since forgotten, the eels at first moved hesitantly in the ebbing tide. The water carried them through an inlet between two islands. It took them under a fleet of oyster boats riding at anchor, waiting for daybreak. When morning came, the eels would be far away. It carried them past leaning spar buoys that marked the inlet channel and past several whistle and bell buoys anchored on shoals of sand or rock. The tide took them close under the lee shore of the larger island, from which a lighthouse flashed a long beam of light toward the sea.

From a sandy spit of the island came the cries of shore birds that were feeding in darkness on the ebb tide. Cry of shore bird and crash of surf were the sounds of the edge of land—the edge of the sea.

The eels struggled through the line of breakers, where foam seething over black water caught the gleam of the lighthouse beacon and frothed whitely. Once beyond the wind-driven breakers they found the sea gentler, and as they followed out over the shelving sand they sank into deep water, unrocked by violence of wind and wave.

As long as the tide ebbed, eels were leaving the marshes and running out to sea. Thousands passed the lighthouse that night, on the first lap of a far sea journey—all the silver eels, in fact, that the marsh contained. And as they passed through the surf and out to sea, so also they passed from human sight and almost from human knowledge.

Estuaries

Where the rivers meet the seas, where salt and fresh waters converge, are the marine crossroads called estuaries. The confluence may occur far inland, where tidal pressures push seawater hundreds of miles upriver, or at considerable distances out at sea, where the greatest rivers finally give up their floods of fresh water. And, since estuaries are defined by salinity rather than by geographical boundaries, part of the estuarine world includes many sheltered bays, sounds, partially enclosed bodies of water or brackish coastal lagoons, bayous and swamps. An area as long and extensive as the stretch of the Atlantic seaboard from Cape Cod to Cape Hatteras, with all of its bays, sounds, river mouths and inland waterways, is classed by ichthyologists and marine biologists as a single estuarine system, the Middle Atlantic Bight.

Like most crossroads, an estuary is a world of constant comings and goings, where migratory fishes pass in their seasons on their way to the oceans or mountain streams, where saltwater fishes come to feed on the uncommonly rich planktonic smorgasbord, where predators lie in wait for whatever the tides and rivers bring their way, whether a single barracuda, poised in the tidal shallows like a lance, sharp nose pointed into the tide, or tens of thousands of bluefish, schooling the waters of an inlet, seeking targets of opportunity.

The stars of the estuaries are the game fishes, the striped bass, the bluefish, the bonefish and the flashy tarpon. None are fulltime residents of the estuaries—they migrate to the high seas, coastal waters and rivers in the spawning season and at other times—but all are dominating presences in the crossroad waters they inhabit through most of the year. Other habitués of the tidewater estuaries are such predators as sharks, skates, needlefish and barracudas, and the mullets, menhadens and scups they prey upon, along with oysters, clams, crabs and lobsters.

The striped bass, a member of the order Perciformes, is the most popular game fish of the estuarine and coastal areas, both for its succulent flesh and its fighting spirit. It is able to survive with no apparent difficulty in either salt or fresh water. It is an anadromous fish, always spawning in fresh or slightly saline water, generally 25 to 200 miles upstream from the tide line. A lone female, bulging with half a million eggs, takes up a spawning position in a fairly turbulent current, surrounded by a group of smaller males; the eggs are released by the female and promptly fertilized by the males in the current, where the eggs drift freely and hatch in two to three days. Within a week the little bass are swimming on their own.

Striped bass are found from New England to southern Florida along the Atlantic littoral and, since their introduction to the Pacific coast in 1879, from Washington's Columbia River to southern California. They travel in immense schools of hundreds of thousands, and individual fish may grow to weigh more than 100 pounds. In summer or early autumn, when the stripers are running in Long Island Sound or Chesapeake Bay pursuing the smaller fishes they prey on, they seem to fill the estuarine world from shore to shore. And then, just as suddenly as they appear, the great schools vanish again—sometimes for years at a time.

Other frequent visitors to the Atlantic estuaries, and also prime targets of fishermen, are the bluefish, smaller but even more voracious than the striped bass. The blues also swim together in great multitudes, which have been likened to wolf packs. Their jaws are armed with needle-sharp teeth, and they will attack anything and everything in their way, churning up the seas in a bloody foam, ripping through schools of menhaden or mackerel in a frenzy of killing, leaving wakes of uneaten corpses behind them and sometimes pursuing their terrified prey right onto the beaches.

The great silver tarpon, a muscular four- to seven-foot prime game fish, is a deepwater fish that regularly immigrates to the estuarine environment, seeking out deep channels to shallow feeding grounds where it scrapes crabs and shrimp from the bottom or wreaks havoc on schools of mullet. It is at home in water from five to eight feet deep. If such restricted, often turbid shallows seem an unlikely environment for such a big fish, the tarpon is remarkably well adapted for it, equipped with a dual system for absorbing oxygen. It has gills like other fish, for breathing under water, and a swim bladder made of soggy, lunglike tissue for absorbing oxygen from the air. The tarpon characteristically surfaces at regular intervals, rolling over in the waves to take in supplementary supplies of air through its swim bladder. Since tarpon are not considered edible, most sport fishermen release them after catching them, often "walking" them through shallow waters until they have taken in enough oxygen to recover their strength and swim away on their own.

Brindle bass

The striper at right has a belligerent look, accentuated by its jutting lower jaw. The male, or bull, is generally smaller than the female—the only external sex differentiation that can easily be determined.

Seven or eight lateral stripes run along the sides of the striped bass (below). The delicate silvery blue iridescence remains when the fish is removed from the water.

Stripers

In the spring, estuaries on both coasts of North America fill with striped bass, or rockfish as they are sometimes called. The stripers are beginning an upstream spawning journey that terminates in a freshwater tributary as far as 200 miles inland.

A female may be accompanied by two or three—or by as many as 50—males as she deposits her eggs. During the egg laying, the surface water is churned up by the frantic activity of the spawning fish in what is inaccurately referred to as a "rock fight." There is no evidence of parental interest after the spawning. The young fish are on their own from the moment they hatch, and by the end of their second summer, the fry make their way downstream to the saltwater estuaries.

The major east coast spawning grounds are in rivers emptying into Chesapeake Bay, Pamlico Sound and upper Delaware Bay. Tagging studies indicate that schools of bass two or more years of age begin to make annual migrations northward and eastward in the spring as far as the coast of New England, probably in search of richer food sources. In the fall they make the return journey, retreating southward as the water cools, and arriving in the Chesapeake Bay region in late November or December to begin a winter of relative inactivity.

The striped bass is native to the eastern Atlantic coastal areas, but was successfully transplanted to the Pacific coast in the late 19th century. Stripers now thrive in west coast waters as official game fish, off limits to commercial fisheries. The Pacific stripers follow spawning and migratory patterns similar to those of the east coast bass.

Old and New

Although the fishes seen on these pages may seem to resemble each other, they represent two extremes on the ichthyological family tree. The ladyfish (below) belongs to the family Elopidae, which consists of the tarpons and their relatives. The elongated, silvery ladyfish have single soft dorsal fins, and pelvic fins placed far back on their bodies, characteristics of the ancestral form from which all modern bony fish evolved. Tarpons range in size from the giant *Megalops atlantica*, which has grown as long as seven feet and weighed up to 283 pounds and which has scales the size of silver dollars, to the relatively diminutive three-foot long, 15-pound ladyfish.

The tarpon snook (opposite), so called because of its tarponlike upturned snout, is not related to the tarpons at all. It belongs to the snook family, Centropomidae, whose members include the Nile perch and the glassfish. The snook's spiny anterior dorsal fin and forward-placed pelvic fins identify it as a well-advanced bony fish.

A menacing-looking tarpon snook (right) scours the water for the fish and shrimp it feeds on. Like tarpons, snooks use shallow estuaries in which to raise their young. The increasing pollution and drainage of these waters by industry is threatening both families.

A small school of ladyfish (below) patrols the shallow waters of the Caribbean for food. When hooked, a ladyfish performs dazzling aerial acrobatics, making it a popular though inedible catch for sport fishermen.

Tarpon

by Zane Grey

Zane Grey's name is synonymous with melodramatic tales of the Old West and of the tough but sensitive cowboys who tamed it. In the following selection from Tarpon, *Grey, himself an expert fisherman, vividly describes the thrill experienced by two men fishing for tarpon and the admiration their valiant prey elicits from them.*

We came to a narrow lane or rather opening in the green bank. Two tarpon were lying on the surface, one with fins out. They appeared to be moving very slightly. Thad stuck his oar in the mud, and taking up my rod he cast the bait right at the very nose of the big tarpon. I watched with immense eagerness and curiosity. And just what I had expected really happened. Roar! Smash! Both tarpon plunged away from there, spreading huge furrows and raising the mud.

"That fellow wasn't asleep," averred Thad. "He was scared. But if he'd been asleep he'd taken the bait for a mullet hopping close. An' he'd sure have hopped it."

"Well!" I ejaculated. "Then you must call this method casting for tarpon?"

"Yes. An' it's the best way, at times like this."

We glided into the opening, to find it a small cove, shallow and quiet, where the wind could not ruffle the water. The bottom appeared to be clean sand.

"I see a buster, over there," said Thad.

"I see one, over here," I replied.

"Yep. There's another in the middle—good big one, too. All asleep! We'll sure hang one of these birds, as R. C. says. Be careful not to make any noise."

Very slowly he moved the boat, in fact so slowly that suspense wore on me. Yet I tingled with the pleasure of the moment. Nor was it all because of the stalking of big game! The little round cove was a beautiful place, reposeful and absolutely silent, lonely, somehow dreamy. A small blue heron flew away into a green aisle where the water gleamed dark in shade.

Not for moments did I espy the big tarpon Thad was gliding so carefully toward. When I did see him I gasped. He lay close to the bottom in several feet of water. But I could see every detail of him. He shone brighter, a little more silvery gold than those we had seen out in the larger cove. His back looked black. I could scarcely believe this enormous shadow was really a fish, and a tarpon.

Thad halted about twenty-five feet distant, and with slow deliberation gently pushed his oar down into the sand. The boat had not made even a ripple.

"Now I'll hit him right on the nose," said Thad, with the utmost satisfaction.

He wound up the line until the leader was within a few inches of the tip; then he carefully balanced, and swung the bait.

"Watch. I'm bettin' he takes it," said Thad.

I was all eyes, and actually trembling. But only with the excitement of the place and the fish. I had not the remotest idea that the tarpon would do any more than wake up and lunge out of there.

Thad cast the bait. It hit with a plop and a splash, not right over the tarpon, but just in front of his nose. It certainly awoke him. I saw him jerk his fins. A little cloud of roily water rose from behind his tail.

Then, to my exceeding amaze, he moved lazily and began to elevate his body. It shone gold. It loomed up to turn silver. His tail came out and flapped on the surface. What a wonderful tail! It was a foot broad.

"He's got it," said Thad, handing the rod back to me.

"No!" I ejaculated, incredulously.

"Sure. I saw him take it in his mouth. . . . So far so good. Now if he doesn't get leary!"

"Oh, he's moving off with it," I whispered, breathlessly. Indeed, that seemed the remarkable fact. The long, wide, shadowy shape glided away from the edge of the shade. I hoped it would move away from the boat. But he was going to pass close.

A triangular wave appeared on the water. It swelled. I heard the faint cut of my line as it swept out. I saw it move. My eyes were riveted on it. I pulled line off the reel and held my rod so it would run freely through the guides.

What an impossible thing was happening! My heart felt swelling in my throat. I saw that great tarpon clearly in sunlit water not over three feet deep. I saw the checkerboard markings of his huge scales. I saw his lean, sharp, snub-nosed face and the immense black eye. All as he reached a point even with me!

Then he saw the boat, and no doubt Thad and me standing almost over him. Right before my rapt gaze he vanished. Next I heard a quick deep thrum. I saw a boiling cloud of muddy water rising toward the surface.

"He saw the boat!" yelled Thad. "He's scared. Soak him!"

But swift though I was, I could not throw on the drag, and reel in the slack line, and strike in time to avert a catastrophe. I seemed to freeze all over.

The very center of that placid cove upheaved in a flying maelstrom and there followed a roaring crash. A grand blazing fish leaped into the sunlight. He just cleared the water, so heavy was he, and seemed to hang for an instant in the air, a strange creature of the sea. Then the infinite grace and beauty of him underwent a change. His head suddenly became deformed. The wide gill-covers slapped open, exposing the red. He shook with such tremendous power and rapidity that he blurred in my sight. I saw the bait go flying far. He had thrown the hook.

With sounding smash he fell back. The water opened into a dark surging hole out of which flew muddy spray. With a solid, heavy thrum, almost like a roar of contending waters, the tarpon was gone. He left a furrowed wake that I shall never forget.

Slowly I reeled in, unmindful of the language of the usually mild Captain Thad. On the moment, as I recovered from what seemed a stunning check to my emotions, I did not feel the slightest pang. Instead, as the primitive thrills of the chase and capture, and the sudden paralyzing shock of fear and loss, passed away together, I experienced a perfect exhilaration.

Something wonderful had happened. I had seen something indescribably beautiful. Into my memory had been burned indelibly a picture of a sunlit, cloud-mirroring green-and-gold-bordered cove, above the center of which shone a glorious fish-creature in the air, wildly instinct with the action and daring of freedom.

Most of the 100 or so species of mullet (left) have muscular, gizzardlike stomachs that are equipped for grinding down the food they filter out of the muddy sea floor. They have unusually long digestive tracts, and a 13-inch fish may have seven feet of intestines to digest the small plants and animal matter it ingests.

Schooling Patterns

Roiling estuarine waters in warm, temperate seas often signal the presence of schooling mullets. Although these may appear to be random groupings, the mullets are actually aligned in precise—though constantly shifting—relationships to other individuals in the school. There is no consistent leadership, and a continuous rotation takes place in the formation as individual fishes change position, but the general schooling pattern and direction are consistent. Individuals toward the rear of the group constantly break away, forming smaller subgroups that sometimes swim for a while away from the main school but eventually re-form and rejoin the main thrust.

Ichthyologists speculate that the oxygen supply toward the rear of the formation may dwindle to the point where it will not support the needs of the trailing members, causing the fragmentation and regroupments. As the school moves through the water, one mullet will frequently station itself behind another, conserving energy by riding in the other's wake. If the backwash becomes too bumpy, though, the rearward fish may abandon its free ride and swim on its own. Such shifting serves to confuse predators attempting to get a fix on vulnerable targets, and the schooling allows individuals to combine foraging efforts—making use of the group effort in locating rich sources of the vegetable and animal matter that mullets eat.

The lemon shark is distinguished from other sharks by a distinctive profile: Its dorsal fins, unlike those of most sharks, are almost equal in size, and it has a broadly rounded snout. One of the lemons below is eating a bonefish, and lemons also consume crustaceans and will readily take a hook (left). Sport fishermen regard them as feisty game fish.

Middleweight

In an order that includes the biggest fish in the sea, the lemon shark is a middleweight, growing to a maximum of 11 feet as compared to the great whale shark at 70 feet or the two-foot cat shark. On the U.S. Navy's "shark danger" list the lemon ranks near the bottom—not nearly as bloodthirsty as the man-killing great white and mako sharks, though guilty of occasional recorded attacks on bathers.

Taking its name from the often yellowish color of its skin, the lemon shark is a member of a family with the ominous designation of requiem sharks. The other members include the deadly tiger shark, the blue shark and the reef shark, and the requiems as a group are the largest family of sharks. The lemon shark is an inshore, shallow-water fish, inhabiting sounds, bays and brackish bywaters, and often congregating around docks from the Carolinas to northern Brazil.

Coastal Waters

The waters that ebb and flow in the runnels of a tidal flat and the 600-foot depths that mark the outer edges of the continental shelf might seem to belong to totally different worlds. Nevertheless, these limits define a single watery region that ichthyologists have called coastal—to distinguish it from the true ocean—and it contains the most diverse population of any environment inhabited by fishes.

The coastal region offers such fertile ground for fish life partly because it coincides with the continental shelf. Scarred by valleys and canyons—many of them formed by glacial action in the ice ages, others scooped by rivers long since drowned by rising sea levels—the shelf is a variegated underwater landscape. With its heights and depths, and its differences in temperatures and pressures of water, available light and nutriments, the shelf is rich in layers of sediment that are full of food for crustaceans, mollusks and other creatures. These, in turn, attract and nourish a veritable bouillabaisse of fishes—from grunts to rays.

Of the lesser known among this enormous range of animals—which also includes such universally known fishes as cod, halibut and herring—is the bonefish. Mobile in its habits, the bonefish lives most of its life in coastal waters, but is most conspicuous in its invasion of the shallows—a favorite feeding ground where it nevertheless feels exposed and vulnerable. "It is on the clear flats under a high sun and in scant inches of water," writes one observer, "that the bonefish becomes the gray ghost, the suspicious shadow and the racing wake."

From the bright glare of the shallows to the shadowy regions where the shelf plunges off into the abyss, there is always some sunlight filtering down to the bottom. To offset their visibility, most bottom-dwelling coastal fish are camouflaged—matching the plants, rocks, pebbles and sand of the bottom. Perhaps the most curious practitioners of this form of protective adaptation are flatfishes, the order Pleuronectiformes, which not only take on the texture and colors of the sea-bottom environment, but have also flattened themselves to conform to its contours. Flounder, plaice and halibut are well-known exemplars of this approach to two dimensions, and all have evolved so that only one of their flattened sides faces the water's surface. Both eyes and sometimes the mouth are placed on the upward-facing side.

Most flatfishes are fairly sedentary, but the giant among them, the halibut, lunges from the seabed especially at night in active pursuit of crabs and fishes. In their search for food, halibut—which can grow to lengths of nine feet and weigh up to 700 pounds—travel enormous distances. In one experiment, a tagged halibut was caught 1,200 crow-flight miles from its starting point after a journey of 240 days. The halibut's fecundity is in scale with its size and energy: a big female spawns up to two million eggs.

Just as voracious as the halibut (though considerably smaller), even more mobile and up to four times as fecund is the cod—a legendary fish credited with a major role in building the Portuguese and Spanish empires and making possible the great age of exploration in the 15th and 16th centuries. Cod, which cover the entire northern coastal range, are found in huge concentrations on the Grand Banks of Newfoundland, where their food supply—shellfish of various kinds and cuttlefish—is rich. Cod like their water cold, between 32° and 49° F., and will move northward or downward if the local temperature rises too much for comfort.

The herring, ranked with the cod as among the world's most economically important fish, also favors cold water. Herring prefer the deeper regions at the edge of the shelf, but they will retreat before any warming currents and make their way toward the coasts. So accessible during the warmer months from the shores of northern Europe, herring have always meant wealth to the people of that region. In the early 9th century, Charlemagne founded Hamburg as a fortified port to defend the herring fleet, and a 17th century war between England and the Netherlands was fought mainly over control of the Dogger Bank, a great North Sea herring fishery.

Today, the importance of fish such as the cod and herring as sources of food for the whole world is greater than ever. Yet the great northern seas, where such fish were once found in apparently inexhaustible numbers, are being depopulated as trawls up to 124 feet wide are towed slowly through the depths. Ships capable of catching and storing 5,000 tons of herring stay at sea for two months at a time. Realization that such overfishing may be endangering world food supplies has been slow in spreading beyond scientific circles. But some observers, at least, have guessed it for a long time. An old English saying sums it up: "If you drop a shilling into the water near the Dogger Bank, it may not be fished up on the same day, but someone is bound to haul it up the day after."

Hundreds of schooling gray snappers (left) swerve to avoid an intruder. Gray snappers have the typical profile of their family, with sloping snouts and strong teeth. They often weigh up to three pounds. The elegant yellowtail snapper (below) is more slender than the gray, growing to two feet in length and weighing four to five pounds.

Snapper Commune

The 250 species of snappers that comprise the family Lutjanidae are all inhabitants of warm seas. The gray snapper (left), also known as the mangrove snapper, is found from the middle Atlantic states southward to Brazil. Like most of its family, the gray snapper is a schooling fish. Each school not only consists of fish of the same species but also comprises a generation of individuals of comparable size. The school's uniformity heightens the effect of its precision movements. Although scientists are still analyzing the schooling process, it is known that there is no one leader in the group. Rather it is thought that as one member of the school perceives danger and starts to move away from it, it transmits signals that are instantaneously picked up by the rest of the school. This results in their sudden and simultaneous reversals or changes of course, always moving in the same direction as a unit.

The slender, graceful yellowtail snapper (above) is one of the few family members that frequently does not school, traveling instead singly or in pairs. The yellowtail's tail is larger and more deeply forked than that of most snappers, giving it greater speed and maneuverability in the waters of its tropical Atlantic home.

A tiny African pompano, or threadfin (left), floats on buoyant filaments that disappear when it reaches adulthood. Mature threadfins are often identified as Cuban jacks.

Looking like a carving in blue glass, an adult threadfin jack (right) retains only one exaggeratedly long, flexible ray fin on its dorsal and ventral sides.

Schooling, long-finned pompanos (below), which for obscure reasons are also called palometas (little doves) or old wives, are pelagic fishes that frequent coastal waters of the western Atlantic and also venture occasionally into the surf.

Pompanos in Profile

Streamlined and with the deeply forked tails that are the hallmark of fast fishes, pompanos are among the speedsters of the world's warm-water coasts. Their striking silhouettes, many with prominent, backswept dorsal and anal fins, are remarkably like those of their brothers, the jacks—so similar that the flashy fishes are often confused. The difference is in the eating: Pompanos are among the most delectable table fish in the world; jacks are poor fare indeed, barely edible and often poisonous.

Their common denominator, apart from similar profiles and appearance, is speed. When hooked by an angler, a pompano will suddenly take off at astonishing speeds. In flight, a frightened pompano will frequently turn on its side and skitter over the waves like a flat stone being skipped across the surface of a pond.

As small fry some members of the family, like the African pompano or threadfin (above), have fantastic filaments that trail from their dorsal and anal fins like pennants in a regatta. These filaments are thought to provide flotation for the baby fishes. As they grow larger, the threadfins lose their trailing threads and their body shapes change so radically that they were long identified as separate species. The silvery common, or Florida, pompano, a game fish of Atlantic coastal waters from Cape Cod to Brazil, has relatively short fins but is just as quick as its cousins.

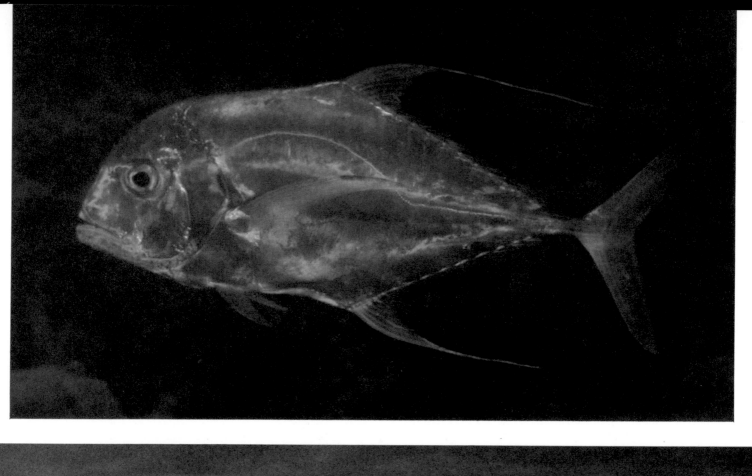

A group of silvery kelp perch (right) swims among the flowing weeds from which they take their name. Kelp perch grow to be about eight inches long. They feed on sandbugs, fish eggs, clams, crabs and other fish. Kelp perch are one of 20 or so species of surfperch, most of which are found in temperate coastal waters of the Pacific from Baja California to Alaska.

At Home in the Kelp

In the coastal waters of the Pacific Ocean, tangled beds of the tall seaweeds called kelp grow like aquatic jungles and provide a home and refuge for many colorful fish, some pictured here and on the following pages. The kelp perch (right) is one species of the surfperches, so called because most of them are found in the coastal surf.

Ranging from British Columbia to Baja California, surfperches are of special interest to scientists because they are one of the few marine teleosts, or bony fish, that bear live young, a fact first noted by the renowned naturalist Louis Agassiz in 1853.

Surfperches mate during the spring or summer, but the male's sperm remain separate from the eggs within the female's body for varying lengths of time, delaying fertilization until the following fall or winter. The young, which may number less than four or as many as 90, develop in the female, where they are nourished mainly by the ovarian fluid that surrounds them. The young perch are born in the spring. They reach sexual maturity so early that frequently they begin breeding almost immediately after birth.

An immature garibaldi (left), with its blue-spotted, gold-colored body, and an even younger, bluer relative poke among the rocks and kelp along the California coast. As they grow older, garibaldis become solid orange in color. The 12-inch fish is the largest member of the tropical damselfish family and one of the few to adapt to temperate water.

The mottled coloration of the giant kelpfish (below) enables it to blend in with the aquatic weeds among which it lives. Growing to a length of up to two feet, it is the largest member of its family, Clinidae.

The male California sheephead (above) is readily distinguished from the female by its strikingly banded, purplish-black and red body. Females are usually a solid dull-red color. Notorious for their irascible natures, sheepheads are ferociously territorial, each male appropriating his own kelp-covered realm, which he defends against all intruders.

Blennies with the Fringe on Top

The blennies and their kin are a large and almost bewilderingly versatile suborder of fishes. Most are small, scaleless or scaled deepwater bottom dwellers, inhabiting tropical or temperate waters. Some swim in northern and arctic waters, still others are amphibious, clambering out of the water onto tide-washed rocks and even hopping around on mud flats.

Some blennies, like those shown on these pages, grow odd, branched headdresses, which may take the form of bushy eyebrows, cockscombs or coral-like tiaras. Their purpose may be to take the measure of hiding places, probe into rock holes for food or to lure small fish and other prey. Though there are other differences between males and females, such as pattern coloration, both of the sexes are fringed, and in some species the fringes apparently serve a purpose in courtship.

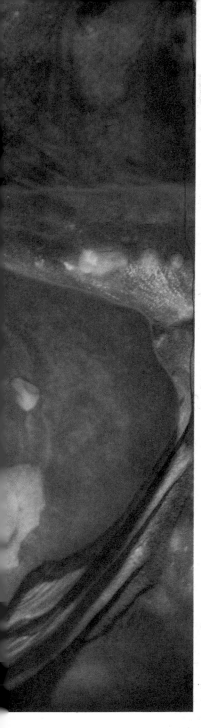

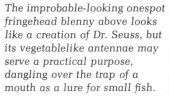

The improbable-looking onespot fringehead blenny above looks like a creation of Dr. Seuss, but its vegetablelike antennae may serve a practical purpose, dangling over the trap of a mouth as a lure for small fish.

The undulating coronet of the yellow fringehead blenny (right) provides a superb camouflage, blending in with rocks and coral formations of the bottom dweller's home territory.

With its brown and black spotted skin, the coiled young wolffish at left has a certain salamandrine beauty that it will outgrow when it reaches adulthood.

"Gold" teeth protruding from its upper lip, the scarred and wrinkled old curmudgeon opposite has the typically disgruntled countenance of an aged wolf-eel.

A pair of adult wolf-eels guard a mound of eggs in an aquarium (below). The eggs are a quarter inch in diameter; the mound is a perfect sphere.

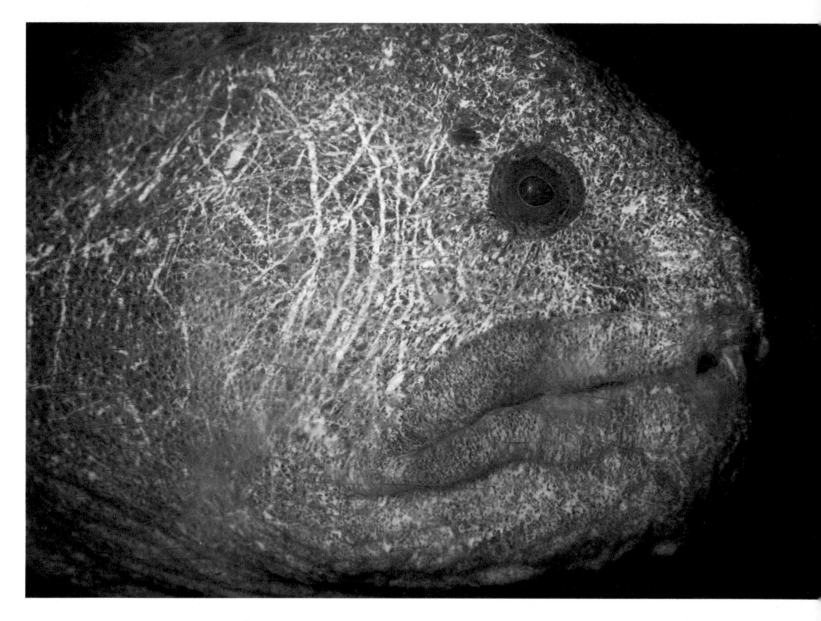

The Sea Wolves

Most members of the blenny suborder of fish are small and highly colorful, among the most beautiful of all fishes. But within the family circle are some members that most people would regard as ugly; by blenny standards they are also whoppers. These are the wolffish and wolf-eels, a group of nine species with tapering tails, oversized heads, formidable teeth capable of crunching the shells of mollusks, and dispositions to go with the teeth. The Atlantic wolffish is the largest of the nine species, growing to a length of six feet eight inches and weighing 40 pounds.

Wolffish are often dredged up in the nets of trawlers, and fishermen have learned to be wary of them, for once on deck they are capable of biting through a wooden pole and of delivering a nasty wound. The wolves of the sea are hardy fish, inhabiting temperate and cold waters right up to the Arctic Circle, and subsisting on a diet of hardshelled mollusks, crustaceans, whelks and mussels, which they crush with the thoroughness of cement mixers and consume, shells and all. As far as mankind is concerned, the redeeming feature of the wolffish is its highly regarded flesh, which is delicious. But, typical of the contrary ways of blennies, there is one species, *Anarhichas latifrons*, that is of little commercial value because its flesh becomes flabby as soon as it dies.

Food for the World

A staple food fish of the world since ancient times, the cod has probably launched more fishing fleets and caused more mini-wars over the right to exploit its teeming habitats (one recent clash was between Great Britain and Iceland in 1975) than any other fish. Most true cods are heavily concentrated in the North Atlantic, though the nonrelated Antarctic cod lives in the Antarctic Ocean. Oceanic, bottom-dwelling creatures, they often need a means of recognizing one another in the murk of their deep habitat. Some have glands that contain luminescent bacteria, and in some the swim bladder is equipped with a drumming muscle that causes a grunting sound; both are useful signaling devices.

The closely related haddock (below) is also found on both sides of the North Atlantic. Formerly discarded from cod catches, haddocks are now recognized as important food fish and are one of the principal quarries of Atlantic bottom fishermen. Female cod and haddock can produce eggs in the millions, which drift with the ocean currents and produce larvae in two to six weeks. After several months, the fish descend to the ocean floor, where the two species dwell together amiably.

The Atlantic cod (above) has a characteristic speckled pattern, a light stripe along its side and a small whiskery barbel on its chin. Its upper jaw protrudes noticeably beyond the lower one, and both jaws are studded with small teeth that make short work of such smaller schooling fishes as herring.

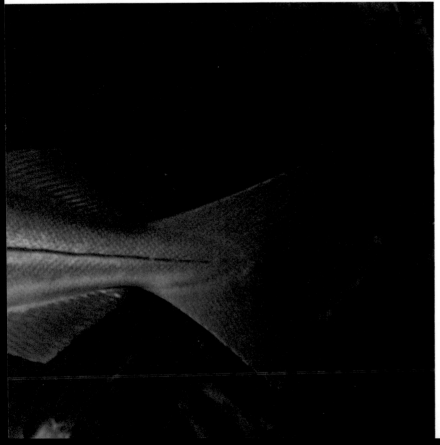

The haddock (left) is distinguished by the large dark mark, called "the thumbprint of St. Peter"—for the Biblical fisherman—above and behind its pectoral fin. Its delicate dark purple and gray coloration is striking, and it closely resembles the cod, except for the black lateral line.

101

When a flatfish's bottom-facing eye begins its migration to the other side, in some species the mouth also begins to move around to the top. The resulting twisted mouth gives this flounder (left) the pained look typical of almost all flatfish.

Flatfishes, like the flounder at right, are voracious hunters, and will camouflage themselves on the bottom (overleaf) when looking for the fish, crustaceans and sea birds on which they feed. When close enough, they pounce with mouths wide open.

Like all flatfishes, the sanddab at right is able to move in different ways. To lift itself from the bottom with a burst of energy it squirts water from its gills. To "walk" along the bottom it undulates its long dorsal and anal fins from front to back. And to swim away from the bottom it simply flexes its body from side to side, just like any upright fish.

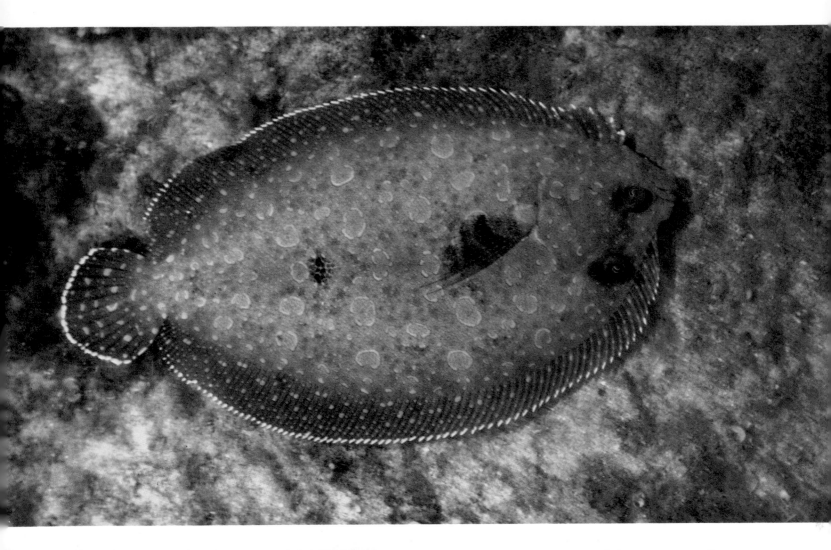

Seagoing Pancakes

Flounder, turbot, halibut, sanddab, plaice and sole are all Pleuronectiformes, or members of the flatfish family. These pancake-shaped bottom dwellers live and breed in all but the coldest waters.

A flatfish hatchling looks like any other fish when it is born, and it drifts or swims upright near the surface. As it grows, though, the fish begins to lean to one side. Simultaneously the eye on its lower side begins to move up over the head to join its fellow. The fish's body flattens and it sinks to the bottom, coming up near the surface only when feeding or traveling.

All flatfishes make excellent eating, and millions of pounds are caught every year. On the market any distinction between species often disappears, and a "fillet of sole" may actually come from any flatfish, with the exception of the sanddab, a west coast delicacy under its own name.

The turbot above blends so well with the coarse sand and rocks of its bottom home that it is almost invisible. Flatfishes are better at blending in with their surroundings than almost any other fish and have been called the "chameleons of the sea." By altering the color and pattern of its exposed side to match that of its background, a flatfish is able both to hide from larger predators and to disguise itself from its own prey.

The coloring of the sanddab at right already matches its pebbly background, and with time would probably change to match the pebbles' pattern as well. If a flatfish is familiar with the ground where it comes to rest, the color and pattern changes take only a few seconds. If the background is unfamiliar, it will take more time—as long as half an hour—for the fish to make its best effort at camouflaging itself. Flatfishes can improve their quick changes with practice, and though they can match yellow or brown backgrounds most quickly, they are capable of reproducing even pink.

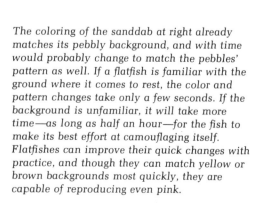

104

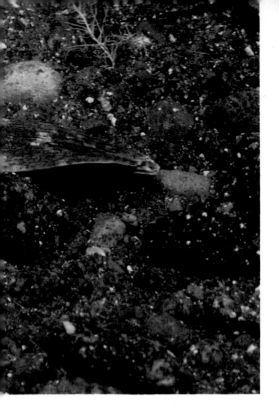

The fish above is a turbot of exactly the same species as the one at upper left. It has already camouflaged itself by imitating the pale color of its sandy background, and blended in even more by wriggling into the sand and flipping extra sand on top of its exposed side. Eventually only its eyes will remain exposed. Flatfishes can only change color and pattern if they are able to see their background. After this initial visual stimulus the fish's nervous system sends messages to minute color cells in the skin called chromatophores. These cells respond by expanding or contracting until their combination duplicates the color and pattern of the background as closely as possible.

Life on the Bottom

If any fish can be thought of as especially fashioned for life on the sea floor, it is the skate. Its body is flattened dorso-ventrally, like a pancake, which allows it to rest as well as to conceal itself in the soft sediment of the ocean shallows. The skate is usually brown, gray or mottled in color and blends well with the bottom, where it spends most of the day resting, buried under a thin layer of sand that it throws over itself by fanning its winglike pectoral fins. In this position the only parts of the skate's body that are exposed are its eyes, situated on the top of its head, and adjacent to them, the spiracles, organs essential for respiration. If this bottom-dwelling creature were to absorb oxygen by taking water in through its mouth, located on its ventral (under) surface, it would also ingest quantities of mud. Instead, clean water is filtered through the spiracles and passed over the gills, which extract oxygen; the residual water flows out through the gill openings on the underside of the fish's body.

When night falls the skate begins to travel, moving gracefully and often swiftly over the bottom with undulating movements of its pectoral fins. It feeds primarily on bottom-dwelling invertebrates, such as crabs, shrimps, snails and clams, which it uproots from the sea floor and crushes with several rows of strong teeth.

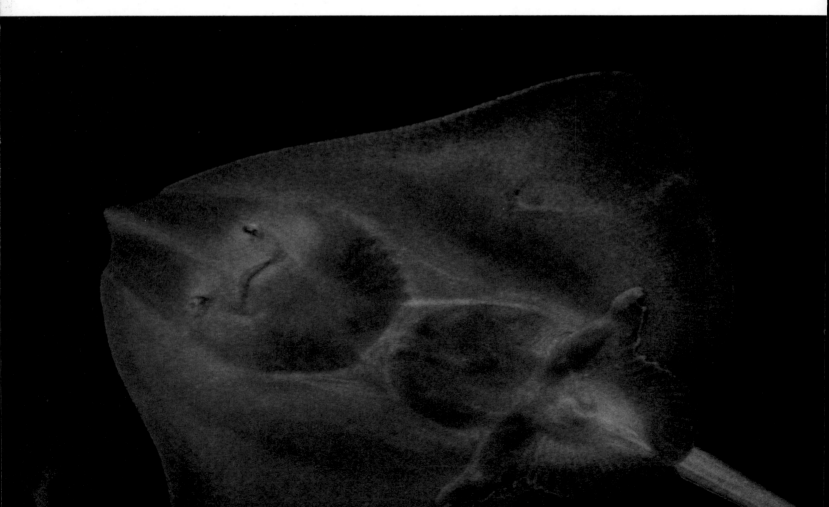

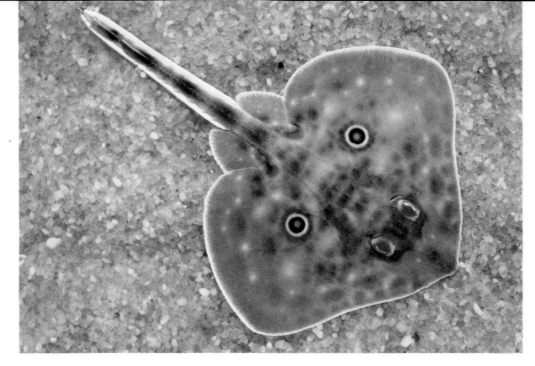

The strikingly marked, coffee-colored roundel skate (left) is distinguished from other common skates by the ocellus, or dark, eyelike spot, on each pectoral fin. The roundel skate grows to be about 21 inches long and is found only in the waters of the Gulf of Mexico from central Florida to Aransas Bay on the Texas coast.

A shoreline creature of North America's Atlantic coast, the little skate (below) has rows of spines that extend the length of its body to the end of its tail and account for another common name, hedgehog skate. Although little skates are most abundant on sandy or pebbly bottoms, they are also found on muddy shoals.

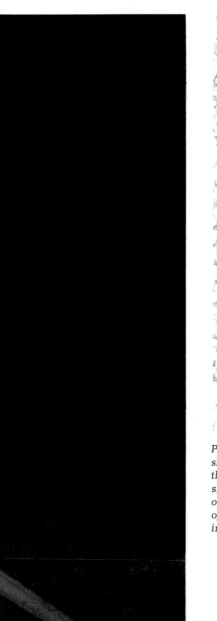

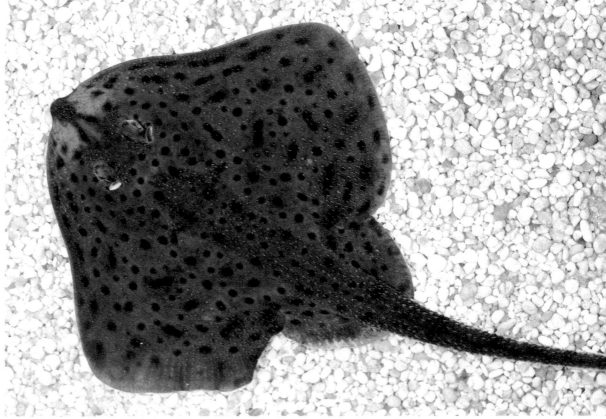

Pectoral fins outstretched, a skate (left) shows off its ventral side as it wings through the water. From this angle the skate's mouth and five pairs of gill openings are visible. The translucence of this skate's skin indicates that it is immature.

The frondlike fins of the sargassumfish help it to blend with the seaweed that gives it both a home and a name. The sargassumfish below uses its prehensile pectoral fins like legs—climbing rather than swimming through its weedy home in pursuit of unwary and smaller fish. Anglerfishes live in tropical and temperate seas.

Fish That Fish

Both the sargassumfish and the goosefish are so-called anglerfishes—a group with a remarkable ability to fish for their meals. What identifies anglerfishes is the first spine of their dorsal fin, which has become separate and highly mobile. Anglers are slow-moving fish, and would probably starve if they had to swim to catch their prey. So instead of going after their meals as most fish do, they lure the food to them. An angler will stay completely still and wave its flexible first spine around in front of its mouth—just as a fisherman jiggles the lure at the end of a line. But the anglerfish never "hooks" its victim. Before a fish can take the bait the angler opens its immense mouth and sucks in the victim with such speed that the human eye cannot follow the movement.

Anglers are able to eat fish that are almost as big as themselves—their teeth slant backwards and prevent even the most vigorous prey from escaping. Anglers vary greatly in size and shape. The goosefish averages two to four feet in length, is flattened from above and below, and is a bottom dweller. The sargassumfish grows only a few inches long, is flattened from side to side and spends it life among floating seaweed.

When not fishing for food the goosefish lets its mouth gape and relaxes the "line" between its eyes (below). If hungry, the fish will settle on the bottom, shut its mouth and extend its lure—remaining motionless until a curious fish is enticed close enough to ingest. Goosefish are extremely voracious and often eat diving birds.

The Deep Sea

The drama of the ocean's abyssal depths is like none other on earth. At the edge of the continental shelf, generally 600 feet down, the gentle slopes of the shelf give way to plunging undersea cliffs—the longest, steepest escarpments anywhere. In some cases, these declivities slope 100 miles until the bottom of the abyss is reached, as much as 35,800 feet deep. At such depths, the sheer weight of seven miles of water induces pressures of eight tons per square inch—over 1,000 times the pressure at sea level.

Yet although fishes live down in these depths, no more than one in seven species of marine fishes inhabits the dense expanse of water in mid-ocean. Among them all, the great game fishes and the sea sharks of the sunless intermediate depths and of the surface are the best known because they are the most visible and accessible. These "fine, blue-backed species," as one observer has called them, are majestic animals, the fastest, strongest and biggest of the fishes. The giant of them all is the whale shark, measured at 70 feet. The bluefin tuna weighs up to 1,000 pounds; swordfish may reach weights of nearly half a ton and

lengths of over 14 feet; the black marlin has been weighed at as much as 1,560 pounds and measured at 14½ feet. Speeds of 49 miles per hour have been credited to the wahoo, with the bluefin tuna a close second at 44 miles per hour; the marlin beats them both at a speed of 50 to 60 miles per hour. The celerity of such fish is sometimes, though not always, coupled with dazzling agility. Tuna and swordfish have dorsal fins that act like keels to give them exceptional maneuverability: Equipped with similar keels, boat hulls halved the diameter of their turning circles.

In sharp contrast is the life lived in the "twilight zone," 600 to 3,200 feet deep, where the last faint rays of daylight can penetrate, and below. At such levels the diversity of fishes is more than 10 times greater than it is on the surface. But one common denominator of these bathypelagic species is the possession of light organs—cells and body parts that act as lanterns. Each of these luminescent organs, or photophores, generally consists of glandular cells in the skin which, in some cases, harbor phosphorescent bacteria. In other cases the cells manufacture a secretion that

Blue marlin

oxidizes and glows when it mingles with oxygen from the blood; the process generates a cold, bright light.

The function of light organs is largely to enable bathypelagic fishes to recognize their own species, particularly members of the opposite sex. This is important for animals that wander in total darkness and in immense cubic volumes of water where encounters with a fellow creature are rare. The role played by photophores in the sex lives of these animals helps account for the retention of their eyes—in some cases proportionately the largest in the animal kingdom—although the absence of light, as in caves, usually shrinks the effectiveness of eyes and often does away with them altogether. Among the fishes of the mid-depths, both their own eyes and their fellows' light organs also come in handy in the search for food.

The fishes that do not eat one another in this world without sunlight—and therefore without edible plants— need suffer no shortage of food. For all live beneath a constant, macabre shower of corpses and mortal fragments that sift down from above, and some venture aloft to the surface waters at night to take their chances of finding something to eat—or being eaten—there. Paradoxically, the fishes that lie at the very bottom of the abyss have an easier life—despite the water pressure and the darkness (which has robbed some species, though not all, of their eyes). Life on the bottom is like life on the ground, lived more or less in a single plane. A fish need only mosey along in this plane and, sooner or later, it will discover something to eat. To help them find such morsels, many deep-sea bottom dwellers have jaws suspended underneath their snouts, and shovel-like mouths; like so many animated front loaders, fishes called halosaurs and brotulids and rattails can scoop up the soft ooze of the bottom and capture burrowing invertebrates. But rattails also dart in pursuit of swimming prawns and fishes, aided by sensitive organs that can detect the movement of an animal in the darkest water. And the tripod fish, perched on two pelvic fins and a tail fin, rests on its undercarriage like some intergalactic pursuit ship, waiting for prey to pass—a perfectly adapted survivor in the earth's vast inner space.

Oceanic Athletes

The spectacular sailfish, along with the spearfish and the marlins, compose the family Istiophoridae, commonly called billfishes. The name refers to the elongated, spear-like snout that identifies them, a weapon that is used to stun prey by slashing randomly through schools of fishes such as mullets and pilchards, and also may be used to spear larger prey like tuna.

All billfishes also have long dorsal fins with many rays. This structure is particularly dramatic in the sailfish and accounts in part for its popularity as a mantelpiece trophy. Sailfish are also favorites of sport fishermen because they can attain speeds of up to 68 miles per hour and put up a good fight, complete with aerial maneuvers, as they lunge from the waves.

Sailfish were once divided into many species, but they are now classified as a single species. The largest is the Pacific sailfish (below), which has reached a record length of almost 11 feet and a weight of 221 pounds. The Atlantic sailfish (right and opposite) is approximately half that size. It is the Atlantic form that has been studied most thoroughly by scientists, who have noted that beginning in the spring these sailfish migrate northward, probably in pursuit of the smaller fishes that are moving into the warming waters. The reverse migration takes place with the approach of autumn.

A hooked Atlantic sailfish (left) puts up a fight for its life. Even though the handsome fish gives even experienced anglers a run for their money, the sailfish is considered the easiest to catch of all the billfishes.

An Atlantic sailfish thrashes wildly as it tries to break free of the line around its bill (right). Like most pelagic fish, the sailfish has a dark-blue back and light-colored belly for maximum camouflage at the surface.

A Pacific sailfish (below) shows off its acrobatic skills. The sailfish's streamlined body and large, lunate tail identify it as one of the faster fish in the sea.

Denizens of the Deep by Philip Wylie

Philip Wylie (1902–1971), best known for Generation of Vipers, *his searing indictment of American motherhood, moved to Florida in his later years and became a passionate fisherman. In his book,* Denizens of the Deep, *he describes his fishing experiences with a rapt exuberance that is far removed from the slick, hard-bitten style of his earlier writing. In the following excerpt, Wylie tells of his first encounter with a blue marlin.*

This substance became reality when the mate, at the controls on top of the cabin, suddenly yelled, "Here he comes—your side, Mr. Wylie!"

And there, indeed, he came. I had a glimpse of a black bill slashing in the purple water behind my bait. I saw the high-standing dorsal. Underneath it was a frighteningly big shadow. A mouth opened—it seemed as big as a coal scuttle. My bonefish was engulfed. The line whipped out of the clothespin high on the outrigger and the big "V" of slack fell into the sea. This slack gives the marlin (as it does the sailfish) the impression that he has stunned his quarry and furnishes him time enough, thereafter, as the boat moves on, to devour what he has hit.

I leaped into the fighting chair and buckled on the harness—just in time. The slack came up and I struck, not with my arms, as one does for sailfish, but with my back and shoulders, across which stretched the broad belt of a harness, fixed to the reel. I struck three times. The marlin began responding immediately. I wished that some of my trout-angling friends who are accustomed to a run across a thirty-foot pool and under a two-foot waterfall could have been there. For my marlin beelined away from the boat, at top speed and without stopping or turning, for five hundred straight yards!

When he did turn, he turned up. At a distance of a little more than a quarter of a mile, he dived into the air, twisting, writhing, falling, throwing spray like an air-launched torpedo and catapulting back into the atmosphere again. Six jumps and he decided to try the straight pull again. The skipper cut the boat around and gave chase. We ran for a mile or more, neck and neck. Or possibly, in that furious mile, I got back a little line. Unfortunately, from the standpoint of the marlin, this one decided on a new course. He took off at right angles, and then I did gain line.

In ten minutes—or fifteen—or twenty—he stopped dead. For five more minutes he lay beneath the tossing surface of the indigo sea and merely shook his head. Every time he shook it, I was lifted out of my seat—and, of course, dropped back with all the force that gravity invests in the sudden release of support. The marlin leaped again. For fifty yards or so he ran along on his tail, throwing a

wake like an outboard racer and eying us bitterly. Then he bored straight down.

The *Sea Queen* was ten miles offshore; the Gulf Stream ran deep there. But this particular marlin sounded until he hit the bottom. That fact we were able to prove later for, on his belly, were deep scratches from the coral reef.

Fighting a marlin that has sounded is something like trying to keep a mineshaft elevator from falling deeper into its pit with a winch that slips. The strain is incessant, the weight tremendous, and whenever you reel a few precious yards of line onto the spindle, something gives, and down the fish goes again, taking all you gained, or more, or—if you are lucky and the fish is tiring, perhaps a little less. I have hooked marlin that went down a couple of thousand

feet and stayed there, dogging around. I have fought them there for hours, through thunder storms that snapped down lightning on the surrounding sea, through stinging rain squalls, into darkness—fought them, and lost them there, when the line finally broke or some sharp edge of reef cut it in two.

This marlin, destined to be my first, gave up hunting for safety in the pitch-dark ocean abyss after half an hour. He began a return to the surface that beat my fastest efforts to reel and came out within fifty yards of the boat. Here you will begin to see why I said that marlin are insane.

The big fish reconnoitered us by means of a few fast-breaking leaps and by greyhounding around our stern. When I got a tight line on him again, he charged the boat.

There is a considerable dispute amongst not only anglers but scientists as to whether marlin take this rare step on purpose or merely in their random, wild way of getting about. I hold with the "on purpose" school. But whether with intended malice or with mere blind indignation, the marlin poised himself on the surface, seemed to aim, and came at us like a skip bomb. He caught the *Sea Queen* squarely in the stern, too. There was a shock. The sound of sea and wind was louder than what must have been a sharp crack. For the marlin's bill point rammed into the mahogany planking of the stern and some three inches of it broke off and stayed there, like a spike, driven deep.

This outraged the fish; he lathered the sea in our immediate vicinity. Something like an hour and a half had passed, by this time. I knew I was shot. But, at lucky long last, I was battling a blue marlin that was even more spent. I began bringing him in the final, rugged hundred feet or so. The mate made a snatch at the leader wire and got it. The skipper ran to his side. Both waited for a favorable cant of the *Sea Queen* and then, suddenly, my marlin's head showed over the gunwale, his broken bill held by rippling human muscle. The despatching club was applied and in he came.

During the battle I had taken it for granted that I was fighting a monster—a five-hundred-pounder, or a bigger one. Maybe even a record-breaker. On the scales, the fish weighed 237 pounds. Not exactly a baby marlin, but a child marlin, at best.

Sociable Heavyweights

If the world at large knows the tuna fish as a mundane sandwich spread, ichthyologists and sport fishermen recognize it as one of the most dramatic, impressive oceanic fish. The tunas are related to such fast and feisty game fish as the bonito, skipjack, wahoo, Spanish mackerel and albacore (the "chicken of the sea"). Tunas are the heavyweights of the mackerel family, and the biggest member, the bluefin, regularly achieves weights of 450 pounds and sometimes 1,600 pounds. For all their heft, bluefins are among the fastest of all fish, racing through the seas at top speeds of 40 to 50 miles per hour.

The tunas are gregarious, traveling in schools of as many as 100 when they are young, in groups of a dozen or so after they grow larger. They swim in every ocean, and travel prodigious distances in their annual northward migrations in quest of the herring, mackerel and other schooling fishes they feed on. They also cross the oceans from west to east and vice versa: By tagging individuals, scientists have determined that tunas cross the Atlantic from New England to the Bay of Biscay, and the Pacific from California to Japan, although the reason for such deviations from their normal north-south migratory routes is something of a mystery.

Glinting like silver submarines, the tunas (left) show the almost scaleless skin and smooth contours that contribute to their remarkable speed. In some species, the dorsal fin folds down into a groove for further streamlining.

The streamlined profiles above look somewhat like those of tunas, but the handsome fish are actually yellowtail amberjacks, very distant relatives of the tunas. They occur in the South Pacific and are highly esteemed as game fish.

Streamlined

One remarkable feature of the dolphin, an open ocean fish of both the Atlantic and Pacific, is its contrasts in color. Its dorsal fin and back are the same deep blue-green as the ocean, and its lower sides and forked caudal fin are a golden yellow. There seems to be no function, such as camouflage, for the fish's brilliant coloring; it serves only as a lovely form of decoration. When the dolphin is taken from the water its entire body surface ripples and flashes. Its tapering body gives the dolphin a shape that is as unmistakable as its coloring. With this streamlining a dolphin creates a minimum of friction and turbulence in the water, and it can swim 40 to 50 miles per hour.

There are two species of dolphins—the common dolphin, or dorado, and the pompano dolphin. The dorado is the larger of the two, and the male dorado develops a steep, rounded forehead as an adult. Adult pompano dolphins are frequently mistaken for immature or female dorados because of their smaller size and more tapered forehead.

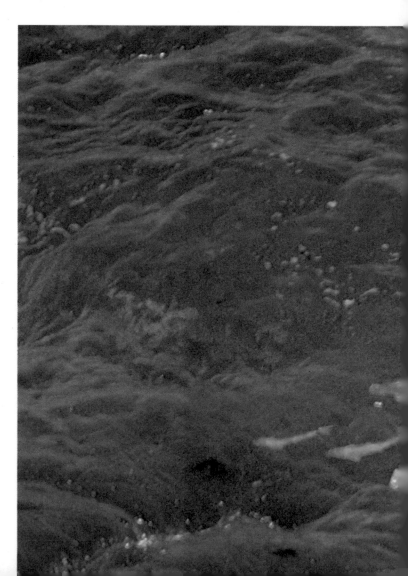

A dolphin hurls itself out of the water (above). In pursuit of its favorite food, the flying fish, the dolphin occasionally leaps, but usually it stays in the water, following the shadow of a fish and grabbing the prey when it reenters the water.

The sex of a full-grown common dolphin can be determined by the shape of its forehead. The male at left (foreground) has a high, rounded forehead; females have foreheads with a more gradual slope.

Dolphin swim near the surface (below) in a school, a form of group behavior common to the young. Seen from above, their outlines blur and merge with the deep blue of the water, making them look more like opalescent flashes of light than fish.

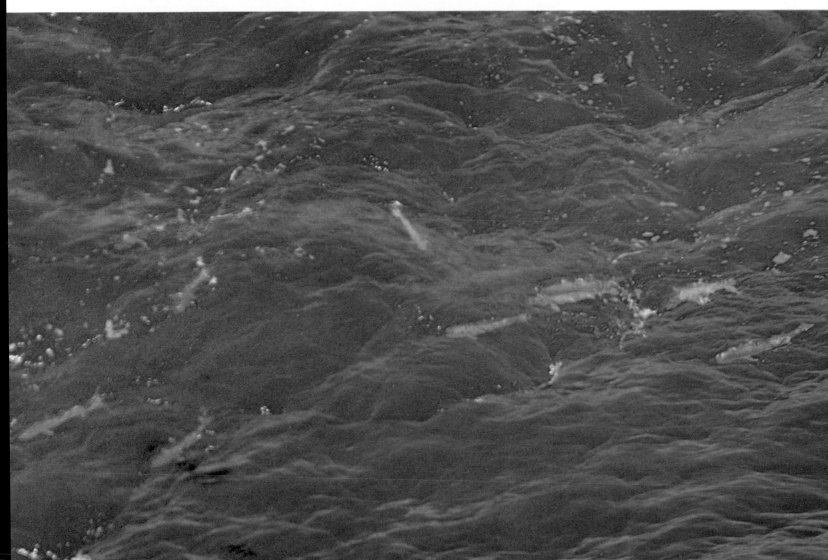

Pilot Lights

Like a tiny spaceship steering a course through an eerie oceanic cosmos, a luminescent hatchetfish (below) casts a cold, phosphorescent light in the eternal twilight zone of the deep sea. As many as two thirds of the bathypelagic fishes, which inhabit the middle depths of the ocean—and some coastal fishes as well—have such bioluminescent systems. When large numbers of them school together, they light up the seas with a ghostly glow.

The luminescent fishes are equipped with several different systems for making their lights. Some employ phosphorescent bacteria that cling to their bodies. Others, using complex light-emitting glands, are able to create their own bioluminescence as a firefly does. Some species of lanternfishes, the headlight fishes, have highly specialized photophores called pilot lights near their eyes. A special muscle permits these fishes to raise or lower the light so that intermittent flashes or strong, steady beams may be cast at will. Another, tinier light organ flashes on first, however, so the fish's eyes can adjust to the brightness before the pilot lights come on.

Since few studies of the luminous fish have been possible (the fish have never been successfully kept in captivity), ichthyologists can only speculate about the precise purposes of the lights. It is believed that they serve as a means of recognizing kindred fish (and possibly of distinguishing between sexes) in the twilight zone. Certain lights are used as lures by some fishes, like the grotesque dragonfish at right, to capture prey. And when a fish can turn on a whole battery of lights, like the hatchetfish below, the bioluminosity may serve to frighten off predators.

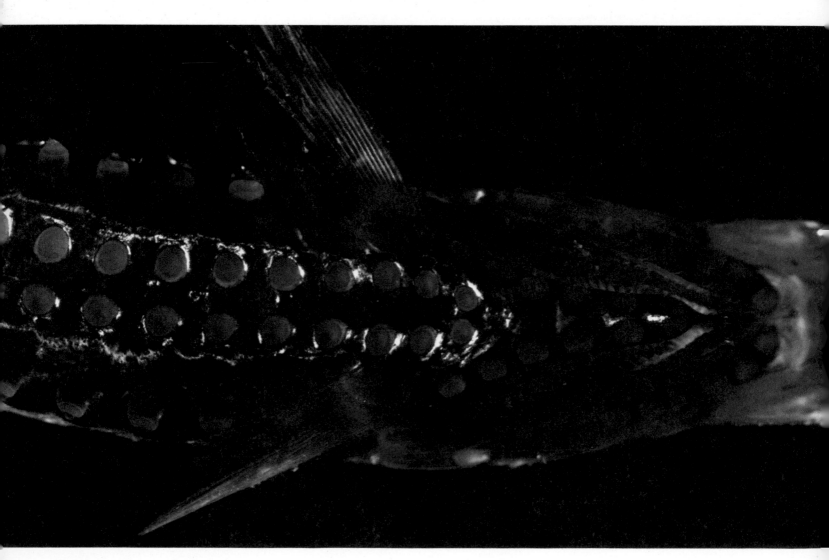

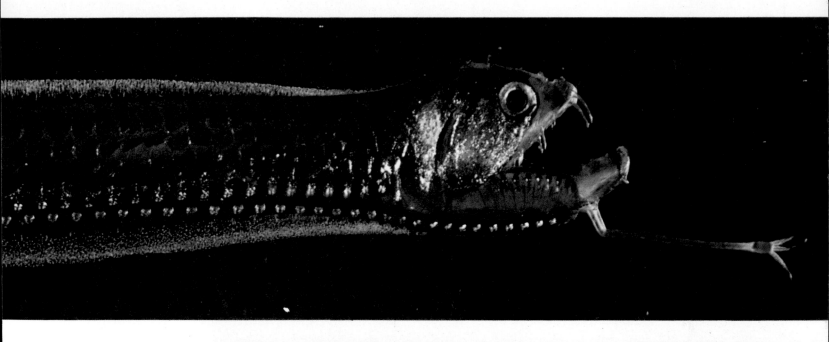

When the highly predacious dragonfish (above) spots a likely victim, the waggling, pronged organ jutting from its chin flashes on a light to lure the prey and its jaws open at an angle of more than 120 degrees. A swift lunge follows, and the prey is impaled and devoured with the speed of lightning.

The ventral photophores of a hatchetfish (left) cast a downward beam in the gloomy depths. In profile (right) the fish resembles a hatchet, with silvery sides that may be a protective device to dazzle its enemies. Although it looks like a hideous nightmare, the hatchetfish measures just a scant three inches.

Outlined and studded with lights, a viperfish (overleaf) reveals its wickedly curving saber-teeth, which it uses to skewer prey. When the foot-long monster prepares to attack, its whole skull tilts up on the end of its spinal column.

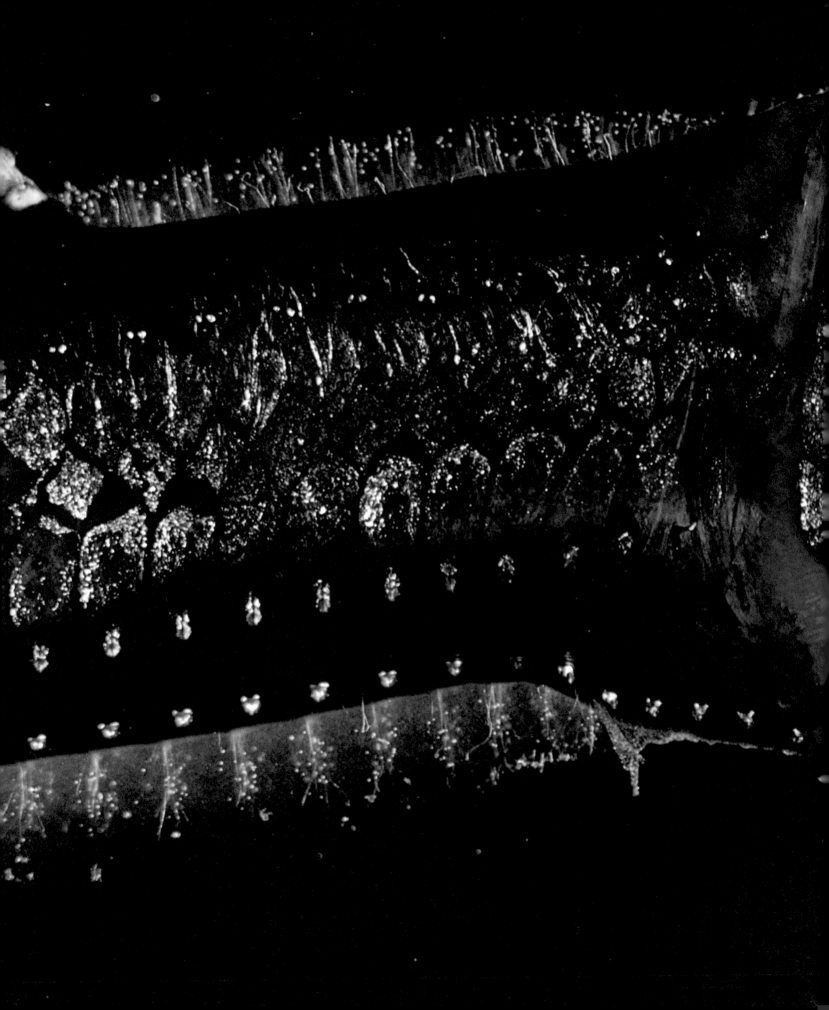

Credits

Cover—J. Foott, Bruce Coleman, Inc. 1, 5—T. McHugh, Photo Researchers, Inc. 6–7—R. Waples, Sea Library. 17–19 (top)—Glenn Lau Productions. 19 (bottom)—T. McHugh, Steinhart Aquarium, P.R., Inc. 20–23—Glenn Lau Productions. 24—J. Hookelheim, Dallas Aquarium, Sea Library. 24–25—B. Kent, Animals Animals. 26–27—T. McHugh, Steinhart Aquarium, P.R., Inc. 28–29—B. Kent, Animals Animals. 30 (top)—T. McHugh, Steinhart Aquarium, P.R., Inc. 30–31 (bottom)—J. Hookelheim, Steinhart Aquarium, Sea Library. 31 (top)—R. Kinne, P.R., Inc. 33—Entheos. 34—G. Gibson, P.R., Inc. 36–37—T. McHugh, Steinhart Aquarium, P.R., Inc. 37 (bottom)—J. Burton, B.C., Inc. 38–39 (top)—N.M. Hauprich, P.R., Inc. 38 (bottom)—H. Reinhard, B.C., Inc. 39—R. Kinne, P.R., Inc. 42—J. Hookelheim, Steinhart Aquarium, Sea Library. 43—J. Burton, B.C., Inc. 44—H. Reinhard, B.C., Inc. 45 (top)—T.. McHugh, Steinhart Aquarium, P.R., Inc. 44–45 (bottom)—Glenn Lau Productions. 46—T. McHugh, Steinhart Aquarium, P.R., Inc. 47—Tom Stack. 50—Glenn Lau Productions. 51—R. Kinne, P.R., Inc. 52–53—K. Lucas, Steinhart Aquarium, Sea Library. 55–58—Entheos. 59 (top)—L.L. Rue, III, Animals Animals. 58–59 (bottom)—J. Munroe, P.R., Inc. 60—J. Foott, B.C., Inc. 60–61—(top) Entheos; (bottom) J. Foott, B.C., Inc. 62–63—J. Foott, B.C., Inc. 63—L.L. Rue, III, Animals Animals. 64 (top)—Entheos; (bottom) J. Foott, B.C., Inc. 65—Entheos. 66–67—M. Stouffer, Animals Animals. 68–69—E. Rogers, Sea Library. 70–71—J. Burton, B.C., Inc. 75—T. McHugh, P.R., Inc. 76—T. McHugh, N.Y. Aquarium, P.R., Inc. 77—R. Kinne, P.R., Inc. 78–79—S. Keiser, Sea Library. 79—Bruce Coleman, Inc. 81—Glenn Lau Productions. 82–83—R. Kinne, P.R., Inc. 84–85—Gil Drake. 87—D. Doubilet, Animals Animals. 88—M. Timothy O'Keefe, B.C., Inc. 89—R. Evans, Sea Library. 90 (top)—C. Ray, P.R., Inc.

90–91 (bottom)—R. Abrams, B.C., Inc. 91 (top)—R.H. Johnson, Sea Library. 92–93—S. Earley, Sea Library. 94–95—J. Foott, B.C., Inc. 95 (bottom)—D. Powell, Sea Library. 96–97—T. McHugh, Steinhart Aquarium, P.R., Inc. 97—R. Kinne, P.R., Inc. 98 (top)—T. McHugh, Steinhart Aquarium, P.R., Inc.; (bottom) T. McHugh, Pt. Defiance Aquarium, Tacoma, P.R., Inc. 99—S. Spottee, P.R., Inc. 100–101 (top)—T. McHugh, Pt. Defiance Aquarium, Tacoma, P.R., Inc.; (bottom) R. Kinne, P.R., Inc. 102—R. & V. Taylor, B.C., Inc. 103 (top)—N. Sefton, P.R., Inc.; (bottom) T. McHugh, Steinhart Aquarium, P.R., Inc. 104–105 (top)—S. Earley, Animals Animals; (bottom) K. Lucas, Sea Library. 105 (top)—S. Earley, Animals Animals. 106–107—F. Lane, B.C., Inc. 107 (top)—J. & D. Bartlett, B.C., Inc.; (bottom) N.Y. Zoological Society. 108—R.C. Hermes, P.R., Inc. 109—R. Kinne, P.R., Inc. 111—Gil Drake. 112 (top)—Glenn Lau Productions; (bottom) F. Baldwin, P.R., Inc. 113—Glenn Lau Productions. 118—Bob Evans, Sea Library. 119—Ben Cropp, Sea Library. 120–121 (top)—Gil Drake. 121 (bottom)—J. & D. Bartlett, B.C., Inc. 122–125—Oxford Scientific Films.

Photographs on endpapers are used courtesy of Time-Life Picture Agency and Russ Kinne and Stephen Dalton of Photo Researchers, Inc. and Nina Leen.

Film sequence on page 8 is from *Sharks Near Shore*, a program in the Time-Life Television series *Wild, Wild World of Animals*.

ILLUSTRATION on page 9 courtesy of the Pierpont Morgan Library. The illustration on page 11 courtesy Musée Condé, Chantilly, from Photographie Giraudon. Chart on pages 12–13 and illustrations on 14–15 by Enid Kotschnig. Drawings on pages 40–41 by Chas. B. Slackman; those on pages 114–117 by John Groth.

Bibliography

Bigelow, Henry B., and Schroeder, William C., *Fishes of the Gulf of Maine*. United States Government Printing Office, 1953.

Böhlke, James E., and Chaplin, Charles C. G., *Fishes of the Bahamas and Adjacent Tropical Waters*. Livingston Publishing Company, 1968.

Breder, Charles M., Jr., *Field Book of Marine Fishes of the Atlantic Coast*. G. P. Putnam's Sons, 1948.

Department of the Interior, *Endangered and Threatened Wildlife and Plants*. Federal Register, July 14, 1977.

Eddy, Samuel, and Underhill, James, *Northern Fishes*. University of Minnesota Press, 1974.

Everhart, W. Harry, *Fishes of Maine*. State of Maine, Department of Inland Fisheries and Game, 1950.

Farrington, S. Kip, Jr., *Fishing the Pacific*. Coward-McCann, 1953.

Gold, Margaret F. and John R., "Golden Trout in Trouble." *Natural History*, December 1976, p. 74.

Hardy, Alister, *Fishes and Fisheries*. Houghton Mifflin, 1959.

Halstead, Bruce W., *Dangerous Marine Animals*. Cornell Maritime Press, 1959.

Harlan, James R., and Speaker, Everett B., *Iowa Fish and Fishing*. State of Iowa, 1956.

Hasler, Arthur D., *Underwater Guideposts: Homing of Salmon*. The University of Wisconsin Press, 1966.

Herald, Earl S., *Living Fishes of the World*. Doubleday, 1961.

Holcik, Juraj, and Mihalik, Jozef, *Freshwater Fishes*. Hamlyn Publishing Group, 1968.

Hubbs, Carl L., and Lagler, Karl F., *Fishes of the Great Lakes Region*. The University of Michigan Press, 1964.

La Monte, Francesca, *North American Game Fishes*. Doubleday, 1952.

Lanham, Url, *The Fishes*. Columbia University Press, 1962.

Le Danois, Edouard, *Fishes of the World*. George G. Harrap, 1957.

Marshall, N. B., *The Life of Fishes*. The World Publishing Company, 1966.

McClane, A. J., ed., *McClane's Standard Fishing Encyclopedia*. Holt, Rinehart and Winston, 1974.

Migdalski, Edward C., *Angler's Guide to the Salt Water Game Fishes*. The Ronald Press, 1958.

National Geographic Society, *Wondrous World of Fishes*. National Geographic Society, 1965.

Netboy, Anthony, *The Atlantic Salmon: A Vanishing Species?* Houghton Mifflin, 1968.

————, *The Salmon: Their Fight for Survival*. Houghton Mifflin, 1974.

Norman, M., and Greenwood, P. H., *A History of Fishes*. Hill and Wang, 1963.

Romer, Alfred Sherwood, *The Vertebrate Body*. W. B. Saunders, 1970.

Schultz, Leonard P., *The Ways of Fishes*. D. Van Nostrand, 1948.

Simon, Hilda, *Living Lanterns*. The Viking Press, 1971.

Sterba, Gunther, *Freshwater Fishes of the World*. The Viking Press, 1962.

Walden, Howard T., *Familiar Freshwater Fishes of America*. Harper & Row, 1964.

Waterman, Charles F., *The Fisherman's World*. Random House, 1972.

Index